Sacred Road

My journey

Through abuse

Leaving the Mormons

Embracing spirituality

Todd Maxwell Preston

Published by Awakened Healing in 2013.

ISBN 978-0-473-26794-0

Disclaimer
The views and opinions expressed in this book are solely the views and opinions of the author. The narration of any story has the author's perspective and in this memoir it is no different. The greatest care was given in writing the truth even when the truth can be difficult to write.

The author welcomes correspondence by email: azureskythepoet@gmail.com

Acknowledgment
A huge thank you to Gillian Tewsley for her editing expertise: I felt like she was a guide who gently pushed me to articulate the truth through simplicity. Not only a guide but an editor with the ability to know what I was trying to say, and who helped me write even more clearly.

To Maryn, Chloe, Sophie, Kate —
I will always love you, no matter what.
Please never stop questioning . . .

Contents

'Religion murders creativity with a smile,
leaving a vase of flowers to honor your dead soul.'

Chapter 1

New Converts

My father was sexually abused as a boy. I found this out when I was thirty-five years old. Was I shocked? Not really – he was raised with violence and abuse, in a very dysfunctional system. The abuse was accepted as normal, I get that now. The fact that it was treated as normal made it all okay. I'm thirty-six years old as I write my story, it is just a story. I am no longer attached to my story. My story used to be everything, it justified all the anger and rage. I thought that my story was who I was. I offer my story to all who have been abused, also to the abuser, also to those who would like to understand abuse. All who have not yet let go of their story.

All that I went through, I blew out the other side from a six-year spiritual journey. I experienced a financial meltdown. I left the Mormon religion. I also chose to end my twelve-year marriage, in which we created four beautiful sacred beings, my daughters. I share my story for them.

My father was born in Timaru, New Zealand in 1944, the fifth child of seven children. I have heard many stories from my father of the dysfunction that existed growing up as a boy. He told me that he was sexually interfered with – those were the words he used. I suppose in a way he was trying to help me understand why he abused me and my siblings. Mine was physical and mental abuse. Religion didn't exist in his home when he was a boy; the religion would come much later.

My mother was born in Rotorua, New Zealand in 1948. The ocean separated the two of them: my mother grew up in the North Island, my father grew up in the South Island. Her upbringing was very different from my father's, a much more affluent lifestyle. There was abuse also in her home, from her father, though what kind of abuse I don't know. It has never been talked about. Her father was a hard-working, arrogant man who never said sorry to anyone, ever. He went all the way over on a ship to the United States of America, graduated from Palmer Chiropractic College in 1933, then he packed up his few belongings, drove all the way to the West Coast and departed once again on a ship, all the way back to his home country. My mother is the youngest of three, and she was always the apple of her daddy's eye. There was no religion in her home either; as with my father, religion for my mother would come later.

My father left school when he was fourteen years of age. Apparently this was quite normal for the time. The story that stands out to me the most is this: when my father was only ten, his teacher told him to stay after school. Whatever it was that he supposedly had done, it seems rather insignificant now. The teacher told him, 'Preston, you will never forget this,' then he caned my father with his pants around his ankles. I have no idea how many lashings he received that day; I was told he walked home sobbing, with blood-soaked school uniform pants. His parents never said a word about the incident: the teachers were the law back in those days. This helped me understand my father's distaste for any authority figure in his life, especially school teachers. They were second-rate citizens to him.

I never had the opportunity to meet my grandfather on my father's side. He passed away a few years before my birth. I was told he was the mellow, gentler side of the family. He was rather distant and detached from his surroundings. My grandmother, my father's mother, whom I affectionately called Nana, she was my favorite to go and stay with. I loved being around her. She was simply lovely to me. When I was around ten years old, I would go and stay with my nana for a few days. I remember watching her sit in her favorite chair, drinking whiskey and smoking her cigarettes – she rolled her own smokes. She would tap the ash onto her thigh then rub it in with her hand. I always thought this was funny. I would sit in front of her open fireplace and throw bits of paper into the flickering flames and watch them burn. My nana would watch me tenderly and tell me that my dad was such a good boy. The thing I remember the most was how free I felt when I was with her. It was a small moment in time when I was allowed to be myself. It felt so good, even if it was only for a moment. It was very confusing to me how this woman was the mother of my father.

The small town my father grew up in was considered a blue-collar town. The geographical nature of this small town was centered on the bay. The fishing industry was an important aspect of local commerce; also the freezing works, where sheep were slaughtered, employed many of the locals. My father worked there for a short time.

During his adolescent years my father set out on a very destructive path. The pain from the abuse was beginning to rear its ugly head. At some level the abuse had to be buried, but the denial must have caused even more suffering. He was unable to deal in an open way with the abuse that had happened to him as a young boy, and his behavior changed for the worse. There were many alcohol-related accidents – almost twenty major car accidents my father was involved in, in one way or another. It's a miracle he walked away in one piece. My father was twenty-one years old when he met my mother. He was smitten with her beauty. For the next couple of years they met with heavy resistance from my grandfather, my mother's father, who went so far as to send my mother to Australia for a period of time. Apparently it didn't work; my father won her heart. My mother returned to New Zealand, where they later married. My grandfather was not at all pleased with the marriage. Perhaps it was the stark difference between their economic backgrounds: he was losing the control he once felt he had. The years that followed became a constant battle between my grandfather and my father. Moving around the country quickly became normal – my parents moved almost as often as the weather changed. This pattern of behavior continued throughout my own life. My father was running from something, perhaps running from himself and the fear that seemed to control his life.

My mother gave birth to her firstborn in 1969, her first son. My father distanced himself through the bottle, which only escalated the pain of his childhood abuse. This is when the abuse began with my mother. I do not know the extent of the physical violence that existed, but its pervasive energy flowed for many years. It wasn't long before my grandfather arrived to take his daughter and grandson home with him. I was never told exactly why he was there; but the signs of abuse were glaringly obvious. The story was told in a way that put all the blame on my grandfather. I suppose this justified my father physically grabbing my grandfather and throwing him out of their house. I heard this story told many times by my father with a comedic undertone, like it was funny. As a small boy I was unsure why a story like that was funny.

Not long after the incident my father moved their small family to Australia where my mother bore her second child, another son. Who knows what dreams my father had in Australia with a family of four – perhaps putting a little distance between his demons and the dark cloud he couldn't seem to shake. At some level he believed he was doing the best thing for his family; I don't doubt this. He was still running from his abuse, hiding from the wounds, rather than facing them.

It was during their short stay in Australia that my parents were first introduced to the Mormon missionaries. According to my father he had never heard of the Mormon Church before. Initially he had zero interest whatsoever in their message. My mother on the other hand saw it in a completely different light: to her, this was a possible chance at a life without abuse, salvation from a life that she was ready to run from. The rest is history: my father quickly got on board when my mother told him she was leaving the marriage if he didn't investigate the Mormon message. The message was accepted and my parents were baptized into the Mormon Church. This was a huge step for them, being from such different backgrounds and, most of all, with no religious upbringing. The Mormon Church is not just, We get baptized into a new religion; it is, We just gave our whole lives to this religion. The changes were drastic, to say the least – their lives had to become radically different. There was excitement and a pioneering spirit that gave them a sense of belonging to something bigger than themselves. Joining a new community brought immediate comfort, a speedy transformation without doing any personal healing. They now had a whole new identity that formed a new path. Old habits were replaced by new ones, in a stark contrast to their roots back home in New Zealand. They soon returned to their homeland, perhaps with renewed vigor towards a life that held such promise. A third child was on the way – my older sister, the first daughter.

In with all the new and out with the old didn't sit too well with the extended families. In both my mother's family and my father's family, their newfound faith was treated with disdain and contempt. Their new religion caused a great deal of conflict and separation. The conflict must have been very difficult for my parents, living as they did so close to their families.

Their new community family within the walls of the church must have been a huge support to them, compelling them in a way to throw all that they had into the Mormon Church. It was literally their new way of life. It was the perfect storm for converts into the Mormon religion – the shattering of families when joining (and when trying to leave). It is a religion that expects not part of you, but all of you. The controlling atmosphere of the Mormon Church seems to attract individuals who need rigid structures and control in their lives. If you are willing to jump through enough hoops within this religion, it can work really well for some people. Certainly it created the perfect cover for my father to now hide behind.

The Mormon Church has a documented history from its early inception in 1830 by founder and prophet Joseph Smith, who was a charismatic leader and orator. Today the Church preaches a fabricated version of church history with a number of omissions that are quite well known among religious circles. The practice of plural marriage – polygamy – was first introduced by Joseph Smith and was closely used by himself and some of the highest leaders in the early days of building his following. It was practiced only by the male members of the church, and was inconsistent at best. Joseph Smith was married to more than thirty different women, and a few of them were under the age of sixteen. They were called his spiritual wives. He incorporated this into Mormon doctrine as being revelations from God. This later led indirectly to his death in 1844: he was shot by an angry mob who stormed a jailhouse where he was imprisoned for destroying a printing press that published an exposé criticizing his practice of polygamy.

Mormons today are indoctrinated with a history that has fictitiously been rewritten to hide the truth. In other words they do not believe Joseph Smith broke the law or practiced polygamy. Fifty years later polygamy was denounced by the Mormon Church to comply with the federal government and, even more importantly, to gain governmental control of the state of Utah. Mormons continued the practice of polygamy after the official 'Manifesto' in 1890, requiring a second 'Manifesto' in 1904. Today the practice of polygamy continues in the state of Utah by those who see themselves as the true followers of Joseph Smith. The mainstream Mormon Church will excommunicate any known member who practices polygamy.

Fifty years ago leaders of the church preached from the pulpit that any man of Black African descent was a curse from God and that no Black male could hold the Mormon priesthood – the authority to act in the name of God. In 1978 it was changed to facilitate a growing membership around the globe and, more importantly, the opening of a new temple in Brazil – a nation with no way of tracking lineage or bloodlines.

The Mormon temples are the pinnacle of evolution for adult membership: once admitted, strict guidelines, secrecy, and ordinances are entered into. After a two-hour filmed production, watched in white robes and green aprons, an acting devil threatens everyone in the room that, if they do not uphold every promise and covenant, they will be in his POWER. The entire room stands and raises their right arm to the square and promises to lay down their life for the Mormon Church if necessary.

Chapter 2
Birthing of a Bullseye

My father began working directly with the church educational institute on a full-time basis. The institute offers additional education for adolescent Mormon children, as if three hours of instruction on Sunday is not enough. My father must have impressed someone at the top: he was promoted as the new director over the seminary program for all of New Zealand. It was at this time that his ego was in full control of his life. The abuse that he suffered was comfortably tucked away, back into the shadows, like it had never happened.

The new job my father held granted him access to the Mormon hierarchy of priesthood leaders. The church headquarters located in Salt Lake City, Utah would one day become my father's destination. Climbing the Mormon priesthood ladder was easy enough in New Zealand – why not Utah. At thirty, my father was young. His sights were now set. His dream of setting sail to America – and, of course, Utah – and his visions of mingling with the Mormon priesthood hierarchy were no doubt uppermost in his young mind.

I have heard my father admit on many occasions that he felt like his children were his personal property. When did this sense of ownership over his children take place? Perhaps right at the beginning, or maybe when he joined the Mormon Church. It was 1973 when my mother bore her third son and her fourth child: only fourteen months separated my older sister and me. I arrived into this world with a bullseye on my back, or maybe my father painted one on me. For the majority of my life I thought I put it there: I felt that I was the one responsible, that I created my father's anger and rage. My father would often tell me that I had the art of pissing people off. The sad part is I actually believed my father. Why wouldn't I? I had the opportunity recently to ask my mother about her state of mind when she was pregnant with me. She told me that she was depressed: she had only recently delivered a baby, and here she was having another one so soon. Who could blame her? I certainly didn't.

As a baby I was rigid. I wouldn't allow anyone to hug me. I would outstretch my little arms while stiffening my entire body in a gesture of resistance. That keen infant sense must have been aware that my environment was unsafe. Early on I developed a strange habit of rocking my head and my entire body when I went to sleep. I would hit my body against my crib, moving the crib to the middle of the room. My mother would come in and move it back to its original position, to no avail; I would always end up back in the middle of the room. This rocking routine lasted until I was nineteen years old. If my parents or siblings told anyone about my strange comfort, the embarrassment was more than I could bear. My father had this urge to break me of this habit. He would occasionally catch me in the act of rocking and threaten to whip me with a belt. I never actually got whipped for rocking, but the threat left me rocking harder.

By the time I was five years old my mother had given birth to three more children – two more daughters and another son. We were now at the lucky number seven: four sons, three daughters.

I don't remember exactly when the belt was first used on me, but I know I must have been extremely young. My first real memory of school was crossing the street on a field trip without permission from a teacher. I got into trouble for this and was sent to the headmaster's office. He instructed me to sit down. In my confusion I bent over his couch, anticipating the belt. He looked shocked and surprised at what I had done, laughed it off and just talked to me. At the time I was only five years old. That memory gave me the knowledge that the belt had been used on me at a very early age.

Strap was the word my father used – it was the simple label he chose to call our weekly beatings. I have heard my father say that he would whip us as hard as he could, intending that we would not repeat the behavior we were being punished for. He expected that the more suffering he inflicted, the better the chance that we would walk his path that he saw for us. It was as though we should be exactly what he wanted; if we strayed an inch from his version of his truth, the belt was coming out. When my father spoke these words, 'Get in my room', oh god I would panic, my whole world would come crashing inward. The darkness, the deep dark hole would open wide; I had the feeling that I would be sucked right in. There was simply no escape from that situation – my father's rage would see it through. The worst part for me was afterwards, sitting in the loneliness of my bedroom, awaiting the empty approach of my father asking for forgiveness. What choice did I have? What was I supposed to say – no, I don't forgive you? From my perspective that would have been like telling Adolf Hitler I don't like the way you are running Germany. I hated myself for this, god I hated myself. I was trying to juggle my battered soul while knowing that I could not speak the truth.

I do remember there being good times, happy moments even. These were moments that were very difficult to relax in. Savoring any moment of peace held only small refuge from the insanity of control. At a moment's notice my father's rage could spill in my direction. It was like navigating a minefield: navigating safely past a potential mine was the happy, safer times; my father's rage and anger blasting in all directions was me stepping right on a mine. To make matters worse for myself, I couldn't sit still. I was either, jumping, wiggling, shaking or fidgeting. This is not at all helpful to a five-year-old navigating a minefield. I must have spilt my glass of milk or water thousands of times. Unfortunately I quickly fell under the steady gaze of my father – like a watchful cat waiting for the little mouse to make one mistake. I became a very scared, nervous little mouse.

I was a major source of contention between my parents. My mother would take a shaky stand to protect me from my father, but this only caused the bullseye on my back to grow. The fact that she tried to stand up for me made me very thankful for her courage. I saw some of the abuse my mother suffered from my father; hiding my father's violent outbursts must have been difficult for her.

Chapter 3

Baptism by Fire

It was 1979, my parents now had seven children, and we were off to the promised land – the land of Zion, as the Mormons affectionately call it. My father's church relationships opened the door for us to move to Utah. With what was a great deal of uncertainty, my parents made the monumental move to America. For my mother, being taken to an entirely different country must have threatened her ability to leave the marriage: walking out of the insanity and control was now almost impossible. Having the image of the perfect family blended beautifully with our new culture, where image is everything.

Getting on board with my father was not an option; you simply had no choice. Sundays were days I dreaded. I had to wear a small three-piece suit, always with a white shirt. The Mormons love their white clothes – it is their symbol of purity. Once again the focus is always external, never internal. When we were in church it was carefully scripted. My siblings and I simply couldn't move or speak; one look from my father down the pew was all that was needed. Ironically I was scared shitless in church. I would carefully watch the second-hand move around the clock and count how many times it had to go around before it was all over. I must have been about eight years old when I began this practice. It was like I was in prison every time we were in church. I remember thinking, I get a vacation from school; when do we get a vacation from church? The vacation never came, except twice a year when the male priesthood leaders met for four two-hour sessions in April and October every year. This is where they speak to the entire membership of the church worldwide. They carefully throw in a few women to speak as well. This large conference always takes place on Saturday and Sunday. I would hardly call this a vacation from church – it was actually a double dose of instruction.

It was during this time that my father gave me what was one of the worst whippings of my life, for a lie he assumed that I had told. I had been slinging mud against the neighbor's house, using a hollowed-out pipe. I remember the house was under construction – at the time it didn't seem like a big deal. I showed my two older brothers, and they quickly took over the mud-slinging game. My father believed their version over mine, therefore I was hammered with his belt for lying. I hadn't told a lie. In the Mormon Church they have a tradition of giving the congregation the floor: anyone can walk up to the front, grab the microphone and bear testimony. You hear some very interesting stories; but it is also very common for children to get up and simply regurgitate what everyone else has taught them to say. Originality is not encouraged. The whole thing is called fast and testimony meeting, and it happens on the first Sunday of every month. So I got my ass whipped good and hard, the day before. Sunday arrived and it happened to be fast and testimony day. As soon as they opened up the floor, up I went, facing perhaps my biggest fear – my father. I let it rip in front of a few hundred people, all my parents' friends and neighbors. I told everyone that my father whipped me for telling a lie and that I knew and God knew what the truth was. I chose to use the seemingly best weapon I had. Ironically it was my father's favorite weapon that he hid behind, the Mormon Church. I have no idea what was going through the minds of the rest of the congregation – I simply didn't care at that victorious moment. To the best of my knowledge, not one person came forward. No one stepped up – it doesn't matter now, all these years later – but this little eight-year-old boy was screaming for someone to throw him a lifeline. I was so scared, I had no idea what might happen that Sunday afternoon. My father, though, never said a word. I had managed to somehow stay in one piece.

Some of my parents' worst fights were directly because of my father's inability to control his anger towards me. I always blamed myself for their fights, knowing that my mother sticking up for me only put me in his line of fire. I would get that god-awful look from my father, that look that said, this is far from over, we will get back to this later. I thought his anger and rage were there because of my behavior, and it was my fault. As I sit here and write this today it seems so absurd, but I was only eight years old. This was supposed to be my father who loved me. The problem was he never loved himself, so his understanding of love was grounded in control and following a single religious path. This had a lot to do with his childhood abuse, which had been sidelined for many years.

It was now 1980. My fourth sister was born, the eighth child. She was the first child to be born in the United States. My parents were very proud to have their eighth child born in America. It seemed to be a landmark for them. I often heard my mother say, 'We moved to Utah so you children would have a better chance at marrying good partners.' I would think to myself, what was wrong with the girls in New Zealand – were they not good partners for your children? It would take me until adulthood to realize what my mother was really saying: 'This is where all the Mormon girls are.' I wish my mother had just said that, it would have made it so much easier. What is the big deal if someone isn't Mormon? All your family back in New Zealand aren't Mormon, are they not good enough for your own children? Perhaps keeping it in the family applied with marriage: keep it in the Mormon family seemed to be a mantra that only made sense within the culture of control. My father would often say, 'Keep it in the family.' I would think, keep what in the family? That you lose your temper and we get whipped with a belt, is that the stuff to keep in the family? The confusion for a young boy was at times overwhelming.

Ironically, the Mormons always talk about freedom to choose: the term they love to use is 'free agency'. If you choose a different path than their path, it comes with a very heavy price on so many divisive levels. They see their position as being one of righteous indignation: you will come to your senses any time; and until that time, we will treat you with distance and isolation. They're on God's side and you are not, so therefore any action they take is justified in the name of their God. I suppose when you are only concerned with your side, the line that they have drawn in the sand is a mirage. For me, it is a line that leaves out love and freedom, and creates the framework of sides and teams, adding to the fear that is so pervasive throughout Mormon communities.

The memories that unfold over blank pages of innocent childhood draw a distinct pattern of conflict and turmoil. The eighth year of my life was pivotal. This is a big birthday for every young Mormon – the year you are baptized and confirmed an official member of the Church of Jesus Christ of Latter-day Saints. Receiving the gift of the Holy Ghost seemed a welcome and long-awaited comfort and inspiration to a conflicted young boy. My big day arrived: it was my time to get baptized and become a newly ordained Mormon. In Utah culture everyone your age is getting baptized, so not getting baptized is unthinkable. It wasn't the thrilling day I had hoped for – perhaps there was some early rebellion in me. I kicked up a little fuss over my father doing my hair – something that happened regularly; our hair was a part of the all-important superficial appearance – and I got a good hard slap across the face before my baptism even began. After all, it was my father performing the baptism: I wasn't sure if he was going to baptize me or drown me. The slap beforehand caused me to doubt the outcome of a long-awaited salvation. I remember a picture of my father and me – my mother must have taken the picture. My father had his arm around me. My hair is still wet from the baptism. Strangely, I'm wearing a football jersey with the number 8 on the front. That picture floated around for years with the rest of the family pictures, and every time it surfaced I would cringe. God I hated that picture, and that entire day. Twenty-eight years later I would have that newly ordained name removed from the records of the Mormon Church.

Of course there were some good things I learned from the Mormons. One that affected me the most was keeping a good journal. For me it wasn't the most consistent of tasks, still, I toiled away at my affection for writing. It's because of my journal that I recall my father making me and my three older siblings run. I was only nine, my sister was ten and my brothers were eleven and thirteen. My father's intentions began as hope that our exterior would shine brightly. The sad truth is that he had been teased as a young boy – the kids called him Fatty Preston. The ugly childhood teasing manifested into a twisted form of punishment. I had to choose between being whipped with a belt or forced to go on a run. My ability to comprehend the inconsistency of discipline was a struggle. Usually, when my running turned into a punishment was when I didn't get up and say my regurgitated testimony on Sunday. I suppose my father's fear wouldn't completely cross the line with church activities. But where that line was I never really knew: sometimes I got the strap, other times I had to go out on a run if I didn't get up and say what my father wanted me to say. There we would be all in a row as a family. My father would look down the pew at me, the look and nod of the head was sometimes all it took. I would get up and make my father proud. The superficial nature of this routine aligned very well with our new culture. Other times I wouldn't budge, even when I got the look. My punishment afterwards would vary – it was very unpredictable. When I was given an option I always chose the run over the belt – it was much easier for me at that age to jog two to three miles. When I was out on the road running I would curse my father the entire way. I could never understand why I was punished for not speaking to everyone in church. I brought this up to my father a few years ago. It was quickly dismissed, like it never happened. But I have a very simple journal entry from when I was nine years old: 'I didn't bear my testimony today so I had to go on a run.' I don't know why a nine-year-old would lie about something in his journal.

I have little doubt that my father wanted the best for his children. He chose to not look at the fact that his way wasn't the only way. Perhaps he still doesn't see this. The Mormon dogma leaves no room for anything outside of their doctrine. In my family there seemed to be sides that were drawn. I rarely if ever happened to be on my father's side. He was always forming sides; still to this day my father forms camps within his own family. My oldest brother by birthright and through my father's understanding of the Old Testament was the chosen son, which seemed to be a wonderful assignment my father had given him. This must have been very difficult for my oldest brother. Rarely could he do any wrong in the eyes of my father. My mother and my oldest brother became my support from my father. On many occasions they would come to my rescue. Many times their efforts were successful in creating a slight enough distraction to deter my father's efforts in tormenting me, but it could very quickly turn in the other direction. My father's wife and favorite son coming to my aid was more than he could bear. It was at this time that I would get double the abuse. These were extremely frightening times in my young life. My father would say, 'Where is your mother now?' or 'Looking for your older brother?' My eyes would give it all away, scanning the room for help, for someone to rescue me from this monster. I became a master at dodging my father verbally. My father would say, 'Todd, did you do this?' I would reply 'Who me? When? What? Where?' – stalling as long as possible, confounding him the best I could. I realized that it was a shaky dance for me, I was walking a very fine line. Other times I got a more frustrated, violent father.

Chapter 4

Ceramics and Baseballs

Soon after this dark period in my life, we moved. We were always moving – throughout my childhood all the way into my teen years I lived in close to twenty different houses. I always tried to look at each move in a positive way – the opportunity to meet new friends, new experiences; I was always up for a brand-new adventure. Looking back on all the moves we made, I wonder today if my father was running from something, whatever he was running from could have been any number of things. As children you don't ever question anything, I certainly didn't – it is the only life you know, so of course this was all very normal.

When I was in the fourth grade we moved to a new community, only thirty to forty miles away from where we had previously lived. Our new school was very nice, nestled within a small mountain community. Our community was so small that the elementary and junior high were combined, first grade all the way through ninth grade, we all shared this small school. I remember a teacher there had a small ceramic lab where all the kids could purchase a small or large ceramic figure, paint it on your own, then watch with great anticipation as your creation went into the furnace and received its last glossy glow. It was magical for me create my own little piece of art. My oldest brother finished a beautiful ten-inch-tall ceramic eagle. I remember thinking what a beautiful job he had done. My parents were so proud of that eagle they displayed it on top of the refrigerator. I on the other hand had eight small ceramics that were displayed proudly above my bed, on a homemade shelf. I don't remember what the little ceramic figures were; they looked nothing like my big brother's eagle. So there I was one day, nervous energy and all, climbing up the refrigerator to get something . . . My brother's beautiful eagle took off like it wanted to fly. It flew for maybe a second then the entire eagle shattered into a thousand pieces. I was shit-ting myself, thinking, this is not going to go well for me. I had no idea what would unfold that evening when my father got home.

I no longer remember exactly what took place. What I do remember is me as a nine-year-old standing out on the cement driveway with my father, all eight of my ceramics in my father's hands. I don't know who in the family watched other than my mother and oldest brother. Even my oldest brother was thinking, this is too much – I could see it in his eyes. I watched my father smash every one of my ceramics one by one. He seemed so justified in his actions. I honestly was thankful at the time that it was my ceramics and not my ass. Today I realize it was that moment that cracked the brittle little foundation I was standing on: a very large chunk splintered off into the abyss that day. The person you are supposed to trust the most – my father – ripped any trust there might have been in half. It was like he took my psyche and chopped it up into kindling. I was such a splintered little boy, and so scared all the time.

My fourth-grade year ended, thank god. It had been a long year. I had attended three different elementary schools. My father was feeling some guilt, or whatever emotion seemed to show up for him. He decided to take me on a trip with him to New Zealand. He was there on business; it was just me and my dad. It was the nicest my father had ever been to me. Maybe it was the fact that it was just my father and me, with no one else to watch. We spent a couple of weeks traveling around New Zealand, visiting with relatives I hadn't seen in a long time. We ate fish 'n' chips, driving a small van, laughing and joking, my father telling stories to me about his youth. Anyone who knows my father would agree that he can tell one hell of a great story. In the time we spent together my father didn't raise his voice or lose his temper. The time we shared together was very memorable for me. I seemed to relax around my New Zealand family – perhaps it was because they accepted me for who I was. My father seemed different when he was around them, a different that I welcomed. It was like there was a line that he wouldn't cross. I felt safe around my extended family, even though I had been taught not to, as they weren't Mormons. They were the most accepting people I knew in my life. I loved staying with them. My father would leave me for days at a time – I suppose it was a vacation from his watchful eye, a time to embrace a different energy than the rigid controlling atmosphere I was used too. A small trip back home gave me a little window of what life could be like without the Mormons.

Two years later, our entire family arrived back in New Zealand. We moved to a quiet little town not far from my father's family. It was a quaint bed-and-breakfast style of town, a really nice place to live. I was eleven years old, soon to be twelve. Turning twelve was very eventful – a landmark for a young man in the Mormon tradition. This is when your father, by the laying on of hands – often along with other male church leaders – gives you the Mormon priesthood, your first entry into a whole new world of church callings, ceremonies and rituals. The Mormons believe that this is the authority that Joseph Smith received directly from Jesus and John the Baptist, along with other New Testament apostles. So they take it very seriously. As a twelve-year-old you are given the responsibility to pass the sacrament during church. This is broken pieces of bread and small cups of water. I don't remember the day I received the priesthood; it's completely blank. I do remember handing out the bread and water during sacrament meeting. I had watched my two older brothers perform this duty, so when my time arrived I felt like I had finally made it. The duties performed in church as a young man holding the Mormon priesthood continue until you're nineteen years old, when you are fully expected to go on a two-year mission. The pressure to serve a mission starts the moment you can walk. You grow up singing songs about serving the Lord for two years. Piggybanks are filled in the hope that one day you will actually pay for your own mission.

I was fast-tracked to a new public school system. In my first week at my new school I found myself changing into my running clothes inside the gymnasium. Some boys had got into the ball room, and every ball imaginable was flying around – medicine balls, tennis, soccer, volley, basketballs. There were at least fifty boys throwing and kicking all these balls. I remember thinking, while dodging every ball I could, this must be what they do here in New Zealand for PE. Two large doors sprang open out onto the rugby and track field, and all fifty boys were clamoring to get out those doors. I still had only half my clothes on when I saw the gym teacher coming, swinging a large stick, hitting everything he could in his path. I watched as the gym teacher broke this big stick in half on some big kid's ass. What amazed me the most was, this boy was laughing. I narrowly escaped out of the gymnasium that day without feeling that stick hit my own ass.

I was okay with this, it was familiar to me. I could navigate my way safely through this minefield. The minefield of a stick used at school was much easier than the minefield of the belt my father used at home.

I fell into a very comfortable routine. I really enjoyed my new life in New Zealand. My extended family became something of a buffer between my father and myself. There were a few family members who saw the bullseye on my back. They were very supportive. Whenever the opportunity presented itself to stay with family I welcomed it. Back in America I felt that I could never be myself, and there was no extended family. I felt so much isolation being around all the Mormons. There seemed to be a serious lack of authenticity back in Utah, where appearances took precedence over a genuine human connection.

There was a small river with a bridge just on the outskirts of our small town. This became the landmark that my sister and I would have to run to, turn around and head back home. Six o'clock every morning before school for the next year we would make this five-mile trek. This was our little stomping ground. When we headed off on our run, we would curse our father the whole way. There was no choice in the matter, we had to run: it's amazing what you will do when you're in a constant state of fear. There were mornings when I arrived at the bridge, I wanted to keep running and never stop.

Of course during this time we spent in New Zealand, church activities played a major role in our large family. Every Sunday we would drive one hour each way to attend the only Mormon church that was in the area. Membership was very small; we were definitely in the slim minority. The minority factor seemed to tone down the arrogance; the air felt easier to breathe. I recently found a journal entry dated Sunday 19 August 1985. This journal entry sums up a small chunk of my life at that time. 'Today we went to a conference for church, it was boring we had to travel two hours to get there. When we got back I got four straps with just my underpants on it hurt I've got bruises. I got a strap because I disobeyed. I also had to go for a jog and we had to wake up really early to go to the conference.'

It really was all I knew – this was my life and there was no escape. The only possible escape that I saw was a divorce. After some of my parents' worst fights a divorce would be mentioned. There were times when I literally prayed for this to happen: I must have been one of very few twelve-year-olds who wanted to see his parents split up. There was no doubt in my mind what parent I would choose to live with. Holding on to the hope that my parents' marriage would end was usually short-lived; my parents always seemed to work it out – perhaps because of all the children, or maybe my mother's fear left her paralyzed to take any action. I saw it in her eyes many times as a boy, the anguish over my father's treatment of her children.

Of course, three boys were more than enough to take up a good chunk of my father's time. Sport was everything in my family. Basketball, football and baseball: these were the only sports that mattered to my father. My sisters were an afterthought – with grounders, shooting hoop, tossing the football, there was no time left to spend with the girls. Unfortunately they blended into the background. I recall a time back in America, when I was eight, I decided to play Little League soccer. I lasted only half a season: my father and my two older brothers all made fun of me for playing a girls' sport. Needless to say I never played soccer again. It's funny, because my father hadn't grown up playing sports. He certainly hadn't played any of the three he cared so much about.

There was no room for error when it came to sports: we had to be the best. Being in my brothers' shadows was perhaps my only driving force. I desperately craved some positive attention, and striving to be just like them was my goal. Of course my brothers were tall and very good athletes, whereas I was the shortest kid in school, which made my challenge somewhat daunting. I was always there, showing up with clumsy enthusiasm, though the enthusiasm didn't usually last long. Basketball was no big deal – at my age this sport involved very little danger. Perhaps this is why I chose this sport to invest all my energy in, though it's not the sport the shortest kid usually chooses. Baseball, on the other hand, was a sport that suited my physical stature.

Baseball began for me in Little League back in America, at around the age of seven. My father would take his three boys to the baseball diamond, where he would hit us grounders. He would hit the ball as hard as he could. I hated this almost more than being made to go on a run. My brothers didn't seem to mind; in fact one of my brothers loved it. He would say to our father, 'Dad, let's go to the park and you can hit us grounders.' I would hear him and immediately think, shit, where can I hide. Of course I had no choice. The part that made it hell for me was if one of those grounders got past me – meaning my father would make me put my body in front of the ball. To me the ball was moving one hundred miles an hour. If I missed some, that's when my father's threats would escalate. He would scream out, 'I'm going to whip your ass if you miss another one.' I would be immediately yanked out of a game if I missed a grounder, in front of all my teammates, coaches and parents. My father would make me catch some really fast throws right there by the dugout. No one ever said a word to my father; everyone would look down or away like it wasn't happening.

One sunny afternoon in New Zealand my father was hitting me grounders in our backyard. He seemed to be even more aggressive than usual. I was extremely nervous: the last place I wanted to be was fielding his grounders. My mother must have picked up on my father's energy. I remember seeing her standing on the back patio looking very concerned. Apparently I missed a few too many. My father made me stand about twenty feet from him. The first throw came screaming into my mitt; my left hand screamed in pain. I remember thinking, shit, I can't catch these. My father's face was so red it looked as though it might burst.

I managed to catch one or two more throws; but the last one he threw just tipped off the top of my mitt, then the ball hit my nose. Everything went black. I couldn't see, there was so much blood. My immediate thought was, this is a really bad bloody nose. In an instant my mother was there with a rag, holding it to my nose. My father walked off without saying a word. My mother took me to a local doctor, where the truth was left at home. I received six small stitches in my left nostril - the baseball thrown by my father had split my nose. He never said anything to me about the incident. I never really understood the importance of all those grounders.

Chapter 5

Wounds of Awareness

My brief stay in New Zealand would leave a lasting impression on me. It seemed, though, that I had a few more lessons yet to learn. Fighting at school was a strange paradox for me. It was a fine line to walk, one of many fine lines I was learning. Walking such a dysfunctional path, directed by my father, often left me in a state of confusion. From my father's perspective fighting consisted of certain parameters: stick up for your sisters; never start a fight; never be a bully; and last but not least, make sure your opponent is bigger. If any of my fights fell within these parameters I would get my father's approval. I don't recall ever getting into trouble for one fight – I obviously navigated through my father's guidebook on fighting fairly well. Thank god fighting only lasted between the ages of eight and sixteen. During those years anger convinced me that I was tougher than any other kid in school. It was the simple fact that nothing outside of my father scared me; all the rage and resentment were directed in every other direction.

It was well known within my family that I had a raging temper. My father was oblivious to this fact. During my earlier years in school I had periodic outbursts. As well as fighting, I had thrown my desk against the wall, screamed at teachers, given them the middle finger – the writing on the wall couldn't have been spelled out any clearer. Ironically all my acting out in school brought little if any discipline from my father. My father's disdain for teachers gave me some liberty: I exploited it. My behavior was rarely addressed by any of my teachers. I know my mother was called on several occasions. She would directly deal with me – she had become very adept in her ability to keep certain information from my father. Damage control directly on my behalf was something I was well aware of. Because of this my adoration and respect for my mother remained constant.

I had been in a handful of fights, bloody fights. It was as though something inside me would snap: all I could see was my father. How could I face him if I lost? I was usually dragged off some poor boy by a teacher, still wildly swinging my arms. I remember thinking, I can't stop swinging until I see blood. It breaks my heart to write this, but it was the truth.

At twelve years old I finally met my match. Truthfully I don't remember what caused the fight between the two of us. The boy was my age, about the same size. I was shocked: he simply was kicking my ass. There was nothing I could do – it was three punches to my face to every punch I managed to throw. My nose was bloodied and I was scared, just as a teacher broke up the fight. I remember arriving home that afternoon somewhat defeated and extremely unsure. When my father learned of my fight and the fact that I had lost, he couldn't leave it alone. I had no choice: I was on the phone asking this schoolmate of mine to meet me in the park in thirty minutes for a rematch. What happened next I must have blacked out from my memory; I honestly do not recall the unfolding of events. Not even a sliver. I do recall the fear I had in calling this boy, who was much tougher than myself. I know it must sound bizarre, but at the time the rematch for me was a much easier alternative. It was reinforced that day that losing a fight was unacceptable to my father.

It was time to head back to America; our stay in New Zealand was just shy of one year. We didn't know we were leaving the day we actually left. My father struggled to make a decision. Some of my siblings couldn't wait to get back to America. I, on the other hand, had no desire to leave New Zealand. My grandfather tried to persuade my father to stay, but the decision was final – we were on our way back. I remember crying as we drove away from a home I had embraced.

We were now back in America for what turned out to be only a short stay; we returned to Australia and New Zealand one year later. During that year in America I attended two different schools. My father's inability to stay in one place left me scrambling for a soft place to land. My defiance at school reached an all-time high, although it seemed to go unnoticed by my parents. I recognized immediately the teachers who genuinely cared for me. I would make as much effort as possible in their classes. It was perplexing to some that I could be a model student in one class, and in the very next class a destructive student. My heart goes out to all of my teachers, especially to those who showed patience, love and compassion. I am grateful for the unconditional love they showed me and their ability to see past my behavior. They threw me a lifeline that I desperately needed.

Almost all of the Mormon churches have full basketball courts. My brothers and I, along with our father, spent many cold mornings at church, bouncing a basketball. I was in the seventh grade, enduring a very cold snowy winter. One particular evening a few weeks before Christmas, in subfreezing temperatures, the four of us piled into my father's car. It was a regular outing – my father would come along to rebound for my brothers. Realizing that we had left one basketball behind, I, being the youngest, was sent back into the house to retrieve it. Meanwhile my father had decided to show his two oldest sons how his four-door sedan could do double donuts in the icy driveway. While they were engaged in this activity, I retrieved the basketball and bounded down the pathway. It was a very dark night. All I could see were the oncoming headlights: I thought they were coming to pick me up. In a way, that is exactly what happened: I got swept up by the force of the tail-light and bumper. The force of the car knocked me perhaps fifteen feet into a nearby snowbank, where I lay unconscious. I have heard my father tell the story many times: he thought that he had hit the house. It was my oldest brother who said, 'That was Todd', at which point my father abandoned the moving car. My oldest brother managed to stop the car by jumping over into the driver's seat and putting the car in park. My father picked up my unconscious body and put me in the back seat of the car. Panic must have set in. My father said to my brothers, 'Do not tell your mother about this.' Perhaps my father thought at that moment that he could have killed me; perhaps the image flashed through his mind of being behind bars. I remained unconscious for maybe ten minutes. As I slowly came to, my bare legs were cold and a little wet from the melting snow but, amazingly, I still had this basketball clutched tightly under my left arm. That's actually the coolest part for me: I never let go of that damn ball. It would have made any running back coach very proud. My father asked me if I was all right. Of course I replied, 'What happened?' Something serious must have happened, it wasn't every day that my father and two older brothers were looking at me, and looking very concerned. The image of the headlights quickly came back to me . . . To everyone's amazement I had just a small scratch on my knee. I told my father I was fine. We continued like nothing had happened. When we arrived at the church gymnasium I was a little dizzy, but I was able to shake it off and play basketball that night. When we arrived home that evening my oldest brother rushed into the house to tell our mother. I have no idea what transpired between my parents that evening. I seemed fine, so what was there left to say. I remember looking at the large dent and broken tail-light on my father's car and thinking, wow, that was my body that did that. What saved my life that dark evening I will never know for sure; but I do know this: someone or something was looking out for me. I like to think that my angels were there for me.

It may be a little strange that my father didn't take me in to see a doctor for a simple examination. From my father's perspective you needed to be on your deathbed, have a broken bone, or severely needing stitches to go see a doctor. It's just the way it was in our family. It wasn't a philosophical stance my father took; it was the way he grew up. It was that way with staying home sick from school, too – you had to be deathly ill to stay home. If we complained of an injury or any kind of sickness my father would respond, 'Quit being such a bloody Hollywood.' It was his favorite word for a sissy or a pansy. It was always Hollywood this and Hollywood that. I recall throwing up at school and of course being sent home; but even then, when I would get sent home sick, my father would give that look that said, If I could I would send your ass back to school. Trust me, as a boy, if I could have stayed at school sick I would have.

Christmas was usually a tough holiday for my father. He had a difficult time accepting gifts. My mother organized all of our Christmases – if it weren't for my mother Christmas might never have shown up in our home, bless her heart. From the presents, the tree, and of course Christmas dinner, she managed to organize the entire day. My mother's dinners were to die for – usually a giant turkey, mashed potatoes and lots of vegetables, with homemade rolls. I suffered through some very tense Christmas Eves. My father would become extremely agitated; it was almost expected. I remember getting my father a gift for Christmas one particular year. For me it came with some apprehension over how he might react. It was very strange to watch my father fumble his way through the unwrapping of a gift. Perhaps there was an underlying current of discontent towards himself – receiving graciously allows the giver to expand their appreciation of the receiver. It unites the very energy of life itself. I gave my father a small wooden elephant that held toothpicks. I thought it was the perfect gift for my father; he loved his toothpicks. It was not well received. The details of that moment have floated away; I quietly rocked and cried myself to sleep that Christmas Eve. Receiving love unconditionally is hard for someone who hasn't experienced this kind of love: they will do whatever it takes to push genuine love away.

It wasn't long after this particular Christmas, my parents once again packed up their large family and headed back to Australia and New Zealand. I turned fourteen shortly before we left. Australia was our first destination. We stayed in some condominiums right on the beach, in the northeast of Australia. It was a beautiful spot, with a large swimming pool, tennis courts, even a small jogging trail. I have some wonderful memories of our short time there, playing golf with my older brothers and our father, eating good food and lots of fresh, locally grown fruit. This was around the time when the opposite sex came into view. Leaving behind such a repressive culture allowed my eyes to expand in all directions. I immediately noticed, with a great deal of excitement, that some of the women in Australia take their tops off while sunbathing. For a young adolescent Mormon boy from Utah this stirred inner emotions that I had previously been unfamiliar with. Viewing the world in a whole new way opened my eyes to other cultures that allowed some breathing room. My father quickly found a new running route for myself and my three older siblings. It was between three and five miles long.

I had been running with my older sister for at least five years. We bonded, in a way, through all our running together. One day that bond would come full circle. I have learned through the years that when we go through a crisis, there seems to always be a strong female standing up for you. It has always been a woman who has helped pull me through my most difficult times.

As well as all the running over the years, there was my father's fat test. He would make me pull up my shirt, then he would pinch to see how much fat I had on my stomach. It's funny, I always believed I was a chubby kid. Looking back at pictures caused a new realization: I wasn't chubby at all. Between all the fat tests and the running, gives me some understanding: my father lacked the ability to see the humiliation he caused; rather, he was blinded by his fear that he would have a fat kid who would be teased the same way he was teased when he was a boy.

It was during this period of my life that I gained full awareness of the extent of the bruising from all the whippings. I was getting dressed in the boys' locker-room one day at school. A good friend of mine saw the bruising that I was oblivious to. He cried out, 'What the hell happened to you?' I looked at my ass and the backs of my thighs as best I could in the mirror. It was the first time in my life that I had seen the full extent of my punishment. I was horrified: the bruising ranged in color from purple to dark blue and gray, covering both ass cheeks and most of the backs of my thighs. At that moment I was sick; my knees felt weak. I realized for the first time in my life that I had these wounds stamped on me. It was a sobering moment for me, one I will never forget. But the wounds within would far outweigh the wounds I saw on my body – wounds without a name or a face, the scars you cannot see, the kind that linger far too long, sometimes a whole lifetime.

Our stay in Australia wasn't long: our stay anywhere for that matter wasn't long. Our large family headed to New Zealand for an even briefer stay, all fifty-four pieces of luggage in tow. I stayed with my nana and papa for a couple of weeks. Then, disappointedly, we headed back to Utah, arriving in the same mountain valley community we had just left a couple of months earlier. I began the eighth grade, somewhat relieved to be reunited with old friends again. Any familiarity at this point in my life was welcomed and embraced. The lingering familiarity of Mormon culture and my distrust in its artificial display remained. The year before, I was cut from the basketball team at the last tryouts. I was crushed; I remember crying right in front of my peers. What added to my disappointment was that my brother, who was two years older than me, happened to be the star of the team. This certainly wasn't his fault – in fact he genuinely felt bad for me. Growing up, this was the brother I fought with the most. My father often affectionately referred to him as the rock of our family, meaning he carefully followed what the Mormons call 'the straight and narrow path'. I was standing in the shadows of my two older brothers.

My parents were now at number nine: my fifth sister was born in New Zealand during our brief stay. Four boys and five girls – wherever we went it brought plenty of attention, even in Utah. In the Mormon tradition, having a large family is seen as a badge of honor, perhaps as one more notch on the belt, securing your place in the Mormon heaven they call the celestial kingdom. This is the place where Mormons believe they become just like God, creating new worlds and new life with their earthly wife, into the eternities. According to Mormon belief, if you do not make the celestial kingdom in the next life, creating for you individually comes to an end. Most Mormons feel they will not make it, because they are not good enough.

For the next two years we actually remained in the same house. This was a very big accomplishment for our family. We enjoyed a brief moment of security. During this time my father traveled extensively to Australia and New Zealand on business. I welcomed his absence: the celebration for me would begin the moment he flew out of the country. Unfortunately my poor mother would have to put up with a rather unruly teenager. My new short-lived freedom was often more than I could handle. In a way I was liberated from prison. Most of the time my mother would keep my reckless behavior from my father – it was her way, I suppose, of protecting me from him.

In between eighth and ninth grades, my father was absent for what seemed like a good chunk of the summer months. I practiced basketball relentlessly, night and day I would dribble and shoot. Playing one-on-one with my older brother helped my outside shot. It was all I had with him; I couldn't get around him to drive to the hoop, so I had to shoot outside. He didn't go easy on me, which was really good. Being a foot shorter than him helped my ability to get rid of the ball quickly. He was really good and I was very average. It led to a position on the basketball team in my ninth-grade year. I was really proud of this – it gave me a little identity.

Those summer nights seemed endless – I was free to explore all possibilities. I spent the night at my friend's barn that had been turned into a hangout spot. There were four of us sleeping over. There was a small weight-room, a place to sleep, and of course the odd *Playboy* that we managed to find – they were always fought over. A little female nudity helped us explore life outside the control and fear of our religion. Cigarettes and all, we were off to find adventure this particular night. Walking the dark streets of a small mountain community gave a sense of an isolated identity. The stars reflected a portrait of possibility upon our mischievous intentions. Gazing into the galaxy that night welcomed a world of no limits. The world was a whole new freedom we were not familiar with. We smoked what we could – our virgin lungs could only handle so much. The four of us ventured to the only gas station there was. It must've been around one in the morning: the streets were virtually empty, other than a stray dog or cat. A dilapidated barn served up the hay we had conspired to set on fire in the middle of the only busy intersection in our small valley. Gas from the closed-down pumps served our purpose; we managed to get just enough. We were giddy with excitement. With four large bales of hay we created a bonfire right in the middle of this intersection. It was spectacular. We danced around our new fire like wild Indians, until we heard the sirens and could see the flashing lights in the distance. It was time to run and hide.

We sat on a small run-down tractor maybe a stone's throw from the scene we had created, motionless and speechless. We watched with anticipation, and a sense of nervous excitement, the firemen and paramedics slowly put out our harmless fire. They obviously had believed that it was a terrible car accident. We walked back to our enclosed hangout only a mile away, smoked a few more cigarettes, of course boasted of our accomplishment. The next morning when I returned home with muddy shoes and perhaps a little guilt, my mother asked me if I had seen or heard the car accident that led to a large fire. Of course my response was a resounding no, I didn't hear anything or see anything. My mother responded with, 'Did you have anything to do with that?' No doubt my guilt was displayed right on my face. That was the best part about my mother – she never pushed me further. It was dropped. But I was sure then and I'm sure now that she knew all along that I had been involved somehow.

Chapter 6
Independent Struggle

Smoking cigarettes or looking at a *Playboy* were considered evil behavior in my world of religion. I had been taught as long as I could remember that such activities were influenced by the devil himself. Whatever light had been in me before was now gone, until I made a full confession to my bishop and repented of my sins. A bishop is always a male figure, who usually has a normal job in his life but who has been called by God to preside over three to five hundred Mormons in a specific geographical boundary. This is his part-time job that he performs as a service to the church. It is a big responsibility, and the bishop becomes somewhat of a celebrity within his community. It is fully expected of each Mormon member to confess any and all sins to the bishop. This takes place in his office at the local church building. The process of repentance cannot begin until you confess. Needless to say I spent many occasions in my bishop's office confessing. It was a horrifying experience for me, one I fretted over on many occasions. Detailed confessions were expected, especially when it came to the opposite sex. Light petting was the breasts and heavy petting was the vagina. I always thought the word petting was strange, it seemed so impersonal. The impersonal part was the very nature of this culture – keep it all on the surface. This was all I knew so I just went along with it, never being comfortable. Masturbation was considered to be a heinous sin. What fourteen-year-old boy hasn't tried masturbation? I thought I was going to hell for sure. It created such confusion, conflict and fear – a frightening combination with my father's control in my life. You felt like who you are was never good enough; you had to become something they wanted you to become. There was no individual expression: having any original thought that strayed outside their box was cause for massive concern.

My mother gave birth to her tenth and final child, my youngest brother. Almost sixteen years separated the two of us. I was now running eight miles a day, mostly on my own. Ironically it became my therapy of sorts, perhaps even the beginning of running from myself. The demons in my own life became more visible; my anger and arrogance became my new mask that I hid behind. All of the pain was shoved away where no one could see it, not even me.

I began my tenth-grade year in yet another house. I would miss finishing this year in school by three months, when once again our large family headed back to Australia. There I continued my education at the second of four different high schools I would attend. Once again it was a culture shock, going from a Utah high school where ninety-five percent of the students were Mormon to a school where no one knew what the hell a Mormon was. Actually for me it was a welcome change. Being in such an open culture once again made it much easier to breathe. My father was relatively busy with his work, which also helped me feel some genuine liberation. There had been rather long stretches, at times, when my father didn't seem to work much, so he was often present at home and this gave him the opportunity to keep his finger fully on his children's pulse. Church activities continued as normal, although our one hour a day church seminary class was no longer at the public school, the way it was back in Utah. We had to attend this class every morning at six before our regular school began. I was playing on the high-school basketball team and running on the beach regularly – it helped to calm down my nervous energy. In addition my brothers and I spent hours surfing and roaming the beach for hours. It was our backyard, literally. My oldest brother and I spent many occasions sitting on the beach smoking pot and enjoying the sound of the crashing waves. It was a wonderful summer filled with laughter and family gatherings. I was slowly beginning to assert my independent spirit, the best I knew how. I was scared, for sure; it didn't curb the defiant spirit springing to life within me. The first of many defiant stands – that I wouldn't attend certain church meetings – was of course met with violent conflict from my father.

I have the most vivid memory of this. We were in Australia, once again staying in some condos right on the beach. My father told me I was going to a church meeting on a Saturday night. It was a two-hour function just for the male members. I took my first shaky stand that I wasn't going. It quickly escalated to his bedroom and of course his belt. I simply was not bending over at sixteen years old; that path for me had ended. During the violent struggle between my father and me, I somehow I got the buckle across my left rib cage. My mother came in, in a futile effort to rescue me. I was getting punched in the back and chest; my poor mother ended up on the ground struggling to stop my father. I was lifted up by my shirt, against a large floor-to-ceiling window. My father was slamming me against the window, four stories off the ground. I remember thinking, this is it, he is going to kill me. He let me go, then he was doubled over with both hands on his knees. He was completely out of breath. I thought he might be having a heart attack. My mother was crying hysterically. I walked out of the room and directly over to the other condo, where all my siblings were huddled. None of them knew exactly what had happened, but they knew something terrible had taken place. As soon as I saw them all, I burst into tears, those beautiful tears flowed, the first real tears in years.

I felt alive. It was the first time in my life that I had taken a stand against my father. It scared the hell out of me, but I knew in that moment I wouldn't take any more, even if it meant my life. My oldest brother asked me if my father had hit our mother. I replied, 'She fell down trying to help me.' My oldest brother charged off in the direction of the other condo, and I reluctantly followed him. What happened next surprised me. My father had apparently regained his breath, and he charged his favorite son, thinking he was once again coming after me. Instinct kicked in: I bolted for the fire escape, eight flights of stairs. My feet barely touched a single step; I hit every landing going down. No one could have followed me at that speed. I felt out of reach for just a moment. I burst through the doors that led outside to the freshness of light rain that felt healing. My body was battered, I was afraid, yet I was free. I hadn't been followed. The night was dark but welcoming, I was outside, I could run in any direction. No one could hurt me out here. I stood there for perhaps ten minutes alone. I walked over to the nearest light, pulled my shirt up to observe my now aching ribs. To my surprise, I had a perfectly stamped buckle welted to my rib cage. It stung ever so slightly. My adrenaline was surging – I stood trembling with fear and anger. What in God's name was I going to do? This had happened in the name of my father's God. My oldest brother appeared through the same doors I had just come through. He was laughing at the outcome. I was relieved that he was there, yet confused with the laughter. It turned out my brother had gained the upper hand on my weary father, using a headlock to stop his violent outburst. I suppose my brother's laughter had an undercurrent of shock, fear, and triumph. Even so, to me it was no laughing matter. I was sick with fear as to the outcome of our situation. My mother had a small window to aid our relief: it came in the form of a one hundred dollar bill. My mother said warily, 'Go and disappear for a while.' What did that mean? I wasn't sure. In the span of one hour, I had gone from 'You are going to a church function' to sitting on the beach with a twenty-four-pack of beer, drinking with my brother, listening to the consistent sound of the ocean that helped soothe the emotional and physical battering that I had suffered. We returned in the morning; to my relief my father had left for the city for a few days. His withdrawal was needed: separation calmed the pervasive fear that still lingered. My father of course returned after a few days. It was never discussed, it was swept quietly under the family rug.

There was a raging fire that seemed to burn inside me now. Managing this fire of rage and resentment was quickly becoming a full-time job. The mask that I put on felt comfortable. I was walking further away from honoring my unsettled soul. I said to myself, I can handle all of this, it's okay; as long as my mask stays in place, who is going to notice?

Not long after my father came back from his retreat I was asked if I wanted to go to New Zealand to stay with my extended family. I suppose my presence was more than my father could handle. I of course jumped at the opportunity to leave the insanity. Within a week I was on a bus bound for Sydney airport and a flight to New Zealand. I was ripe with anticipation: smoking cigarettes, drinking with my relatives was something a young adolescent from Utah only dreams about. After the violent struggle with a father battling his own demons, releasing me to the wild was a gift that I welcomed. I was sent with a small amount of money from my father, with careful instructions to keep a log of my expenditures. I was happy to do so. My attention to detail was amazing. My father was impressed with my written accounts. So was I: I had managed to drink and smoke almost all of his money, only to replace it with make-believe items from a typical grocery store. For me it was liberation for six short weeks – it was what I needed for the time being.

Taking a stand for the first time in my life to follow my own path would teach me later down the road it would be an extremely difficult journey. I certainly didn't know this at the time, which was a good thing: knowing the journey beforehand can leave the sturdiest traveler retreating in silent surrender.

My family arrived in New Zealand after my six weeks of solitude. I was once again happy to see them. Being spread out among my non-religious extended family had been a good thing. My separation from my family led me to understand that it was okay to be away from them. We would stay for a few weeks then head back to America once again, this time to southern Utah, a place we had never lived before. I would start my eleventh grade at yet another school, my third high school. My two older brothers were preparing to go on their Mormon missions. I, on the other hand, had different plans. I joined the golf team at my new high school. Apparently the golf team had a healthy collection of potheads, which suited me well – in fact my best rounds of golf seemed to be when I was high. I was well on my way to hopefully flying under my father's radar, stoned or drunk. My father's attention was directed towards helping his two oldest sons leave on their respective missions. This was a beautiful diversion where I could fly solo. Of course I took full advantage of my solitude.

It was a short stay in southern Utah that lasted only three months. Soon after my older brothers departed on their missions we moved once again to northern Utah, to a whole new community and my fourth and last high school. For some strange reason it was a difficult high school to make friends. Making the basketball team helped immensely, though. The basketball season was a challenging journey with little reward. It marked the beginning of many emotional and physical setbacks in my life.

My father's business ventures seemed to be at a standstill, which gave him plenty of time to spend at home. It was a dark period in his life, a time of deep frustration, insecurity and financial instability. Our relationship once again reunited with dysfunction. His frustration spilled into anger, which led to some violent conflicts. I still believed within myself that I was the source of my father's constant frustration.

Between work, basketball and school I made myself as scarce as possible. I had my own car that my father helped me acquire a loan for; also a steady paycheck. I was asserting my independent spirit to the best of my ability. I continued to rebel in all aspects of church activities; in fact, one time during a church class when one of my church leaders confronted me about my attitude, I simply told him to go fuck himself. It is such a passive aggressive culture: I left him standing there with his mouth open. As scared as I was of my father I simply couldn't take any more. I felt I was putting my life at risk, yet I was willing to take the physical consequences, whatever they might be.

It was during this period of my life that the nightmares arrived. I would wake up in the middle of the night in a cold sweat. My father would be standing over me with something in his hands: he was going to kill me. It scared me so bad I didn't tell anyone about it. I finally mustered up enough courage to tell my mother. She didn't say anything to me – I don't believe she knew what to say. I never brought it up again to anyone, believing that something was wrong with me. It was a dark and oppressive time. The energy within the walls of my home pervaded almost every discussion. An argument would lead to a violent outburst with my father. I made a habit of never leaving my car keys anywhere other than in my own pocket: this way I always had a chance to escape, with my physical form still intact.

On two separate occasions when the entire family was seated at the dining-room table eating dinner and an argument started between my father and me, the closest object within my father's reach found itself airborne in my direction. A basketball was one of those items. In an errant throw from my father, he managed to smash the chandelier hanging right above a dinner my mother had just prepared. Glass went flying in every direction. The other time he threw a fork at me: thank god I saw it coming and managed to duck just in time. The fork stuck in the wall right behind me. Then he was up, trying to get to me; it was a dance around the table, looking for the clearest path for me to safely make it outside. Moving towards the door, I could feel him breathing down my neck. I managed on those occasions to narrowly escape. I've often wondered what would have happened if my father would have caught me. Would it have been a repeat of the incident in Australia? Would he have pushed it further the next time he could get his hands on me in his violent rage? The intensity was palpable. Once outside he would follow me until he was completely out of breath. Once I was free from his reach, the anger would surge inside of me. I would give him the finger, taunt him as best I could. I would scream, 'Go fuck yourself, chase me down, you bastard.' He and I both knew that he could never catch me outside – my legs were the only leverage I had. Eventually he would go inside I would drive off in my car and disappear for a few days. Usually I would go and stay with a friend. When I returned home, very little if anything was ever discussed about what had happened. It was strange for me that things resumed to some sort of normalcy, especially after such violent outbursts.

Then there were times when my father and I seemed to get along fine. We always talked about the same stuff – sports, the girls I was dating. Rarely if ever did we venture off these two subjects. It was a unique dance between the two of us. Perhaps my father felt a loss of control in his own life, and also in my life. There were times I genuinely felt sorry for him. His life was visibly spinning out of control. I witnessed some of the worst fights that I ever remembered my parents having. In a way I had managed to somehow break through a single protective barrier, not realizing then how many barriers lay ahead for me, barriers that would help set me free and would allow the unfolding of a possible personal destiny.

I began to see the first signs of my father growing weary. It gave me a small window to explore some missing independence. I managed to skip out altogether from almost all church activities. I came and went pretty much whenever I wanted to. My senior year of high school, though, would serve up a few more lessons I apparently needed to learn.

Chapter 7
Two-Year Mission

Believing I had a surefire position on the basketball team, I was unexpectedly cut from the team. I was crushed beyond belief; it was really my only identity at the time. My arrogant, chauvinistic demeanor was silenced for a short while, only to quickly find a new identity in the form of the wrong kind of friends. Drinking and looking for fights – these new friends sought both activities. Fighting for me had come to an end when I was floored by a tough kid much bigger than I was. It must have been exactly what I needed. One punch to the side of my head knocked my head into a brick wall – I later received twenty-two stitches. Oddly enough this schoolmate and I became friends of sorts, not best buddies, but genuinely nice to each other. Was it because he felt bad for me? or was it the crush he had on my younger sister? In fact it wasn't until after the twenty-two stitches in my head that he found out the girl he liked was my sister. It's interesting how the cycle of events unfolds in our lives. That was a great lesson for me, number two that school year. Needless to say that was the last physical fight I was involved in.

I managed to graduate from high school, certainly not with honors. I always considered myself an average student. Maintaining a full-time job my whole senior year and graduating with a B average felt just about perfect. I continued my job that I enjoyed throughout the summer. Driving brand-new cars around and washing them was fun. I was fortunate to have a boss that I liked a lot. He had taken me under his wing. He was the first person I knew in Utah who despised the Mormon Church. He wasn't afraid to offer his opinion on how he felt. I remember thinking that maybe he had a point. He said to me once that Joseph Smith was a buffoon. I had been raised with Joseph Smith being right up there with deity, so to me this was blasphemy. Of course I said nothing, what was there to say – I hadn't ever taken the time to look at my own religion. Who honestly takes the time to look at their religion at eighteen years old? Up to this point in my life I just wanted some space and of course a little freedom. Looking back on it all, I think I was actually a pretty good kid.

Fall that year was quite eventful. My next older brother arrived home from his two-year Mormon mission. My father organized, through a friend, financial aid for me to attend a college an hour and a half drive away. It was the path of least resistance for me, an easy decision: what else was I going to do? I had made it very clear to my parents that I would not be going on a mission. I seemed to stamp this with enough authority that it became somewhat of a non issue. I found myself with my brother as a roommate – the brother who ratted me out whenever he caught wind of any evil I was up to. Prior to his two-year mission, we rarely if ever got along. We fought almost constantly. From his perspective his way was the only way: stay within the boundaries of the Mormon Church and you're on God's side; any other path than this, you're on the devil's side. He actually described it this way to me: he saw things simply as black and white. So I was a little concerned with my new living arrangements, due to our history. I was genuinely caught off guard. His two-year mission seemed to have quieted his old self-righteous judgment. He seemed so much different than before.

Being away from my family caused some introspection into my life. As a Mormon, almost every male friend you have is leaving on a two-year mission as soon as you turn nineteen, not to mention the fact that the majority of girls won't consider dating anyone in college who isn't an RM, a returned missionary. The pressure is palpable. Not going on a mission when you live in Utah as a young man can leave you feeling rejected and alone. At eighteen soon to be nineteen it permeates your thinking – it certainly did with me. Not to mention I always wanted to be like my brothers. I was always in their shadow and would remain so for many years to come.

I had been an avid reader since I was a little boy. I always had a book in my hand, mostly fiction; the

Hardy boys, Judy Blume and Roald Dahl, I read them all. In my room, growing up, I always had a small bookcase with all my favorite paperback novels. If there wasn't a built-in bookcase I would clumsily build one and nail it to the wall. As a young boy and throughout my life I just wanted to be left alone to read my books. It was in my books where I found adventure and freedom; this is where I seemed to soar.

Seeing this change in my brother fascinated me. I picked up every Mormon book I could read. I read these books not once, but two and three times. I had an insatiable desire to soak up information about the only religion I had ever known. My college grades suffered severely due to my change in direction. This would have been cause for major concern for almost any other parent, but not for my parents. I was on the fast track to going on a Mormon mission. Following the path that they believed was the only way for salvation gave me all kinds of support. At the time my decision to go on a mission was all mine. I had asserted enough independence through some tough years. Perhaps it was time to give in to the cultural pressure. I was walking my parents' truth, and they were giving me love and attention. It felt really good. For now I allowed myself to ride the wave of conditional acceptance.

A Mormon mission is an intense experience: two years of your life to anywhere in the world they send you. You leave to the mission training center, where layers of guilt and programming take place. There is no creativity or individualism encouraged. You are taught the same dogmatic shit day in and day out. You are all taught to teach their version of their truth the same way. It is like a three-week seminar on sales and recruitment. You leave believing that you need to convert the world to one way of thinking, one plan that God has for everyone that is on this planet. If the people don't accept your message they have a chance perhaps in the next life; if it is not received there they cannot enter the Mormon heaven. It's all very black and white: this is the way and there is no other way. Reading Mormon books written by Mormon authors certainly didn't level the playing field. It did release me from college, which I was never fully engaged in. It was the perfect excuse to bail out on my education – who would ever question that in this community?

At my interview with my local bishop, I felt compelled to reveal that I had had sex with a few girls. New church policy stated that one year had to pass before you could leave on your mission. Apparently it was retroactive: it had been eight months since my last sexual encounter, so I only had to wait four months before I could leave. In addition I had to go and see a general authority. The Mormon hierarchy consists of a president, who is the prophet, twelve apostles and the quorum of the seventy, which are the general authorities, all consisting of older men. The seventy act as overseers over the entire church membership worldwide. They are all treated like celebrities within the church, received and welcomed like deities. Most of them are very wealthy on their own accord, astute at running a business; many were CEOs, lawyers and doctors before their full-time calling to serve the church. Once in this full-time calling they are paid for their service to the church. As to the extent of their salaries, no one knows.

My interview with the general authority was a brief visit. I remember the whole experience very well. It was a large office, and I felt extremely intimidated. He sat behind a huge mahogany desk. He looked to me to be all of seventy-five years old. The last words I remember him speaking to me were, 'Don't let the church down.' I replied, 'I won't.' I walked out confused; it made very little sense to me. Where did I fit into all of this? The church was more important than the individual. It was one of many small lessons I simply couldn't shake.

All was in order with the proper church authorities. My papers were completed and mailed to the church headquarters. A few weeks later I would receive my mission call. Coincidentally, I was off to the Brisbane, Australia mission, exactly where I had been three years earlier. I was excited – with my state of mind at the time, hell, they could have sent me anywhere. My call was a direct call from God – how could I not go with excitement? I continued my reading, furiously devouring every Mormon mission book, on forgiveness, Jesus Christ, Joseph Smith, their version of church history and more on Joseph Smith, and of course the Book of Mormon. Over the course of two years I would read this book well over thirty times. I enjoyed expanding my knowledge within the confines of my culture. The mission was a carefully scripted program, very well designed to keep all in line. The Mormon Church has had years of perfecting the mission program. Sending nineteen- to twenty-one-year-olds is actually quite brilliant. You are a sponge at that age, absorbing everything they give you. They have a mission guide that you have to study from every day. It instructs you on everything – what questions to ask, how to get the potential convert to trust you, and of course how to get them into the waters of baptism, with a full commitment to give ten percent of their income to the church. It's very well designed and quite effective. A missionary rulebook is also a must: they actually give you a pocket-sized book so you can carry it with you. I carried mine in my front shirt pocket for two years. The rulebook contains everything, from a curfew each evening; never leaving your assigned companion; even a specific day when you can do your laundry and grocery shopping and letter writing. Of course there is no dating of any kind – any sexual encounter would get you a one-way ticket home with the discharge being: dishonorably released. The fear in facing a Mormon culture in this way gives some understanding as to why it rarely happens. Too much is at stake culturally, socially, and within your own family.

I understood that many of the rules were there to keep the missionaries safe. Some of the rules, though, simply did not make sense. For example you could never go swimming in any body of water. You are taught that the devil controls the water; as a missionary the devil will perhaps get you somehow if you ever go swimming. Looking for validation I became a fanatic with all the rules. Most of my companions hated being with me, I took myself and the rules so seriously. Looking back on my behavior and fanaticism has shed a great deal of light. Being raised with so much fear and control in my life, all the structure was a perfect match for my fear, so I embraced it. To my amazement I rarely if ever got homesick. I had assumed that I would – everyone does. That was not a problem for me.

A Mormon mission is mainly measured in the number of converts you bring into the church. Your life becomes statistics, the number of lessons taught, how many potential baptismal candidates you are working with. This information is reported to the mission home on a weekly basis. Within your mission geographical boundaries, you have a mission president who is your leader and who you are directly accountable to. He lives in the mission home with his wife. You are interviewed monthly. The interview is very personal: in fact I was asked every month for two years if I masturbated. Who knows what would have happened if I had answered yes. My answer was always the same: abstinence was a must. Each missionary is expected to perform four hours of service to the community each week. This is where most of my personal growth came from. I had some life-altering experiences being there for other people, especially as that we were not there to convert them to our way of thinking. It was a quiet reprieve from the constant demand to convert the world to Mormonism. It was during delivering meals to the elderly, helping autistic children at school, mowing lawns for those who could not, where I really saw personal growth. A more sincere young man emerged in this setting. Allowing people to be, giving them space, love, support, accepting them for who they are allowed true communication to occur.

Two years went surprisingly fast. I truly embraced the culture and felt a genuine love for the Australian people. Perhaps I felt that I was one of them. My mission was filled with challenges. I encountered along the way many situations of sexual abuse, physical abuse, abuse in all its ugly forms. I felt that I was too young to hear all the ugliness. Perhaps it was picking away at the wounds of my own abuse. I had hidden my wounds so well. I no longer believed that I was wounded, like these beautiful people. I had hidden myself behind an egotistical arrogant mask, held firmly intact from all the religious dogma I was swiftly becoming fluent in. My reading replaced my running, only now I would add more layers of illusions that seemed to comfort me for the time being.

My mission came to a close. I was excited to see my family after two long years. I arrived home to yet another new community: in my absence my parents had moved again. The excitement of being home faded fast. I realized how little had actually changed, if anything at all. I was thankful for the experience, no regrets. I had worked hard to follow all of their rules. Simply put, I had done what the church asked me to do.

Chapter 8

Zigzagging the Straight and Narrow Path

The ensuing months were extremely challenging. I was twenty-one and living at home with my parents. I was now running again, and running a lot of miles. I trained all summer long for my first marathon, that fall. It was a wonderful experience, my first taste of spirituality, feeling a genuine connection to my own inner spirit. The last three miles of the race I cried and cried, they were tears of true joy. Perhaps the first real tears since being pounded by my father at the age of sixteen.

I reluctantly enrolled in college – what else was I going to do? Of course I chose to work with my two older brothers, same trade, same path. It was once again the path of least resistance for me. While I was away on my mission my two older brothers got married, as well as one of my younger sisters. The first grandbaby was also born. My mission president instructed me to get married within six months of being home. That's some serious pressure to a twenty-one-year-old. It's written into the culture: get married as soon as possible. I was struck with fear that I would never find a wife. I had never had a real girlfriend, all through high school. I had been around a lot of different girls, just never committed to anyone. The thought of commitment scared me, although at the same time the prospect of it excited me. Finding a girl to take on a date was the easy part, but my inadequacies along with my insecurities pushed most girls away.

Conflict with my father returned soon enough – it was like it had never gone away. I realized for the first time that whatever direction I was headed in – whether I was going to church or questioning the reality of my life – it didn't matter; conflict from my father was inevitable. At a cultural level, a Mormon girl was the only girl that I could marry. But I went against my upbringing and, over the next two years, I found myself falling for girls who were outside my cultural boundaries. I was struggling to follow my infant inner voice and the call to be free to make my own choices, without the nod of approval from my family.

My freedom came in the form of a couple of Kiwi boys my father had hired to build his house. They were both around my age, and we immediately hit it off. I saw an opportunity to escape, to leave town and my narrow, controlled world. I had the car they needed for a road trip, and I needed a break from the routine of structure and expectations. We were off to Las Vegas, the Grand Canyon – actually no real destination, just finding our way as we went. It was the trip of a lifetime, simply because we had no plans whatsoever – where we landed we stayed. We were given a free room in Las Vegas – it spontaneously fell into our lap; we slept in some girl's college dorm room in Arizona. We even got a picture of ourselves, completely naked, overlooking a deep ravine in the Grand Canyon. To some this may seem a little crazy, but to me, I felt alive. I was free to explore my independent spirit once again.

It was on this road trip that I met a girl from California. She was a few years older than me, and she was everything that my culture rejected: simply put, she wasn't Mormon. There was enough chemistry between us for us to exchange phone numbers. I pushed forward like I was free and wanted to be, but I was still looking for validation from my family and especially from my father. I called her as soon as we returned home, and she immediately booked to come and see me in Utah. I picked her up from the airport and we headed to a small mountain retreat. I was free to be whatever I wanted to be around her. We stayed in close contact over the next few weeks. I flew to California to spend another weekend with her. I met her mother and some of her friends.

Our relationship was met with immediate resistance from my family, even though no one had ever met her. We had been raised to keep it in the Mormon family. What could I possibly be thinking, dating a non-Mormon girl? Our relationship continued shakily until I caved to the pressure. It was my unconscious decision: I heartlessly ended our short relationship. I never spoke to her again. Fear of the unknown had driven me back to my roots; the fear of leaving the Mormons. I had been taught that my life would implode, and I certainly believed it. I broke up with a beautiful woman whom I really cared about, to continue following the straight and narrow path.

Again I came back to the Mormon fold, repented, confessed all my sins to my bishop. One year later I learned that my once girlfriend from California had tried to correspond with me by mail. My parents had intercepted every piece of mail and destroyed it. To this day I do not know what was in that mail. What a violation, and in the cause of what? They were stealing someone's very freedom, 'protecting' them, based on their self-deluded version of the truth. Sadly I wasn't shocked, it all made sense to me. I knew that my parents believed they were doing the right thing. But the question lingered: was it the right thing for them, or for me?

I continued my education while living at my parents', and I returned once again to the church. It was a silent struggle for me, every time I went to church. I never felt like I was where I needed to be, never felt quite at home. It was what I was supposed to be doing, so I would continue to follow someone else's truth, not my own. Deep down I knew this but I wasn't ready to face my demons. I continued dating, never making a connection with any of the young women I spent time with. It was a frustrating cycle. I found myself questioning the sincerity of the people in my culture – which was odd, because I was not real with myself. I was wearing a different mask for different groups of people, following the crowd, blending in, allowing a group to make my decisions. And I was hurting not only myself but others too. I came up with a term for this person I had become: NRM – Not Really Me. I was arrogant and judgmental. Meanwhile, my rebellious spirit remained quietly tucked under the covers, struggling and fighting to scratch at that surface inwardly, knocking at the proverbial door.

In the summer of my twenty-fourth year, I met a beautiful girl from South Carolina. The chemistry between the two of us was instantaneous. Once again, she was not a Mormon. This time around I would ease into the relationship as best I could; and I would remain cautious during our four-month relationship. The lessons I had learned one year earlier taught me to tread carefully. I did not want to break her heart. There obviously was something inside of me that wanted desperately to walk my own path, so I flirted on the boundaries. She was attending college in South Carolina, and had come out to Utah for the summer to stay with her father. We spent a lot of time together, shared some great experiences. She was so easy-going, it was so relaxing being around her. She too completely accepted me for who I was. I, on the other hand, couldn't accept her for who she was: she wasn't Mormon. I desperately wanted to continue the relationship, but I knew that I didn't have the courage to face my own fears within my culture. The relationship continued to blossom. We trusted each other, and she shared herself with me in a way that was open, honest and loving. Sadly I felt that I could not fully reciprocate her gracefulness. We spent our last night in each other's arms, talking, wondering what might become of our relationship if anything at all. I didn't want to let go of her that night, and I felt the same energy from her.

My religion taught me that I had the truth, all of the truth, the fullness of the truth. Others, non-Mormons, don't have what we have – they are lost and in the dark. This bullshit dogma caused division and separation, and I had once again allowed it to swing its bloody axe directly in my path. This time, though, I wouldn't forget how it made me feel, not to mention how it must have made her feel. That was the last time I would see her, she returned to South Carolina, a few letters were exchanged . . . My life was about to change drastically.

Chapter 9

The Mormon Dream

Allowing my South Carolina friend to leave without sharing my true feelings for her gave me a sense of freedom from needing anyone in my life. It was the first time in my life that I felt I was somewhat okay with myself. A small amount of honesty was all I needed. She had shown me how to be honest with myself, by revealing all her human imperfections. I marveled at her courage, while I buried mine with a lie that I wasn't in love with her when in truth I was. I convinced myself so well that I moved on with false bravado.

I had sold my intuition and creativity down the river in exchange for the security in my religion, my perception of safety – the Mormon Church. The whole time I thought that safety was inside my indoctrinated mind, a collection of beliefs that had been handed down to me from my parents. These thoughts inside my head would bring salvation in the future, so I believed. I was too afraid to think my own thoughts. I felt that I needed to cling to them without ever letting go, hoping that their truth would set me free. It could only work for so long.

I had managed to keep love out of my life until now. I became a drifter in and out of the arms of a handful of girls, believing I was in control of my life, enjoying myself, hanging out with a group of new Mormon friends. I was slowly picking my way through college, working on my general classes. My two older brothers had recently enrolled in chiropractic school in Texas. I felt that they opened the door for me to follow in their footsteps again. It seemed like a good profession – our grandfather had enjoyed a great lifestyle through chiropractic. So I lazily headed in this direction, with very little direction from my own heart. I was on autopilot, allowing others and my culture to make my life decisions. I convinced myself that I was the one in control of my life. I am not saying that my direction was the wrong direction; I just never really showed up to take full responsibility.

I had a group of new Mormon friends, and one of the girls took me by surprise. I had helped organize a double date – my best friend with her; me with one of the girls I was dating at the time. It was a fun evening. When we dropped off our dates and said goodnight, my good friend said to me, 'You should ask the girl I was with tonight out on a date.' I was somewhat shocked – I thought she was beautiful, but a little timid. Needless to say two weeks later I asked her out. I was excited, and she was really excited as well. It was as though we were destined to meet. We were like two little children splashing in a muddy puddle for the first time, clumsily running into each other's arms. We were swimming through a culture that demanded you marry young. I brought her out of some of her shyness; she helped me to feel safe. She was the embodiment of the Mormon girl I was supposed to find: it was almost perfect. My parents loved her; she was the first girl I took home that my parents liked. We couldn't be kept apart – we spent almost every day together for the next three weeks.

Of course I asked this beautiful girl if she would marry me. Everything lined up: both Mormon families supported us; we were on our way to eternal happiness. The Mormon Church teaches this doctrine that families will be together forever in the next life only if you receive your marriage ceremony in the Mormon Temple. They teach that you are sealed together for time and all eternity. This is a critical step in Mormon culture: receive your temple blessings with your new spouse. Without this critical step you cannot make it to the celestial kingdom. So it is a huge process that must happen in order to stay accepted within the Mormon community. Coming from two Mormon families, if you do not marry in a Mormon temple, your lack of repentance is on public display – meaning the newly Mormon marriage was contaminated with sex before being married. Admittance to a temple comes with an in-depth interview from church leaders – once again, all male. Here are a few temple interview questions they ask you: a full disclosure of your yearly income each year (this is related to the 10 percent tithe you will pay); if you have had sex or any sexual relations; if you have partaken of alcohol, tobacco, coffee or tea. Everyone knows within a specific church boundary who can go to the temple and who hasn't gone, so once again community influence plays a huge role.

Needless to say we were headed for a temple marriage. We had dated for three weeks, our engagement was three months – we were on the fast track for marriage. It wasn't anyone's fault, of course. A religion that suppresses personal choice and responsibility is not individual freedom; rather the group or organization makes your choices for you. We were living their dream in an unconscious attempt to live our dream. A good word for it is conditioning.

Even though we had both been raised in the Mormon culture, our different backgrounds were challenging. Her family was a stereotypical Utah Mormon family, very quiet, reserved, repressed, rarely offering an opinion. My family on the other hand was just the opposite. We were loud, everyone had an opinion and asserted it in a way that tried to convince anyone that would listen that it was right. This loud style of communication was not at all well received in Utah culture. Confrontation of any kind generally isn't how you make your presence known in Utah. My father pissed off more than his fair share of people, even being a Mormon himself; there was a massive cultural divide. So our parents didn't hit it off too well – especially my father and her father, who could barely be in the same room together. I suspect that their controlling egos collided, revealing an image that mirrored too much of themselves. This led to years of strained communication between my parents and my in-laws.

I questioned on many occasions whether my father-in-law even liked me. I almost didn't follow through with the wedding because of his inability to connect on a human level. He would go for days without even acknowledging anyone's existence. I took it extremely personally. My soon-to-be wife would constantly make excuses for him: 'He is like that with everyone,' she would say. However it was clear to see that he wasn't that way with everyone. If you were in politics or church leadership, whatever charm he had was definitely turned on. At the time I was insecure and always looking for validation outside of myself. Being back in the Mormon fold I thought would bring instant validation. That was what I was looking for – some sort of acceptance outside of myself, anything to make myself feel accepted. This struggle would continue to unfold over the years – my constantly seeking acceptance from an outside source, from the church community that I did not fit into, or from some individual. I was of course not aware of my desire for acceptance. I could accomplish life on my own, do it all myself; I didn't need anyone or anything. I was fine, nothing was wrong with me. There was simply no healing that needed to take place. I had it all under control – just grin and bear it. So I continued with my bullshit optimism and my smile.

Wedding days are generally rather simple in Utah. The ceremony is held inside the temple, where of course only Mormons holding a temple recommend are permitted. A temple recommend is a small-sized card similar to a driver's license, allowing entrance to the temple. Any family members not aligned with your beliefs, even Mormons who are not adhering to all Mormon guidelines, cannot be there for the ceremony. There is a waiting room for these people and for all of the children. After the ceremony and photos there is a luncheon served to close family members and a few friends. It is kept small and intimate. This is followed by an evening reception. The reception is really for the parents – it is their way of sending you off with lots of handshakes and smiles. We stood in a line for a couple of hours, meeting and greeting mostly people I had never seen or met. It was the first time I had seen my new father-in-law turn on his charm. It amazed me how much energy he put into these relationships, when the same energy was never directed towards his new son-in-law or his own children. I had previously perceived this family as the perfect Mormon family, but once again the shallow role-playing was on full display. I feel compelled to say that I too was playing a role: observing it in others was far easier than observing it in myself. At the time my eyes remained closed to the opportunities that presented themselves to me. I had no idea that I was far from ready to examine myself with the same lens I viewed everyone else with, not to mention the extreme judgment and criticism I was so familiar with. An awakening was something I knew absolutely nothing about.

My new journey with my wife began with this perspective – a glasshouse I was closed into, no vacancy available, with plenty of stones to throw. Of course I was very unaware of my habitation and isolation. I had acquired the Mormon dream; everything else should be easy. The comfortable masks I was familiar with would remain, with the addition of new masks. The layering of roles would continue to smother any authenticity that wanted to emerge. I was a traveler in a culture that was well versed in these customs. I would blend in for now. The small flame inside me would remain in the background, flickering with hope that would one day burn bright.

Chapter 10
Birth and Separation

The first few months of marriage were exciting and brand new. Beginning a family together was something we both wanted and expected. Waiting to have children wasn't really an option we ever discussed – it was once again part of our cultural conditioning. By now I already had around six nieces and nephews. Oftentimes I had looked at some of my siblings' families with envy, wanting desperately to have a family of my own, so it was natural for us to expect my wife would show up pregnant one day. On the other hand our different backgrounds proved exhausting and difficult. It became the center stage for some of our early conflicts. Conflict was not a familiar energy my wife was used to. She'd grown up with some conflict with her father, however this was nothing compared to what I was so familiar with. We resolved our conflict with two completely different styles. Mine was, let's talk about it; hers, I don't want to talk. Time and time again I would only alienate her further, with my resistance to her withdrawal, from resolving any conflict we had. My energy and enthusiasm were too large for her reserved nature: I suffocated her.

We pushed on through the drama. What choice did we have? We had just gotten married, we spent four months getting to know each other – how much could two people really learn about each other in such a short period of time? Two short months into our marriage we were expecting our first baby. The opportunity to move to Texas where my two older brothers lived presented itself, faster than we expected. It seemed a risky move to some, but to us it was an early opportunity. We had very little to no support from my parents in moving to Texas. My in-laws gave us plenty of support, which was surprising but welcome. We loaded all of our belongings into a moving van, and we were off. The support we had on the other end of our twenty-five-hour drive gave us the confidence we badly needed – we were on the road to a place that was so distant from what we knew, but we were going to the safety of another Mormon community.

Sharing an apartment with my brother and family came close to dismantling our fragile marriage. It almost sent my wife, pregnant and out of the comfort of familiar surroundings, literally packing. With our living arrangements and being pregnant for the first time, it can't have been easy on her. She simply wanted to go home. The call to the familiar is strong and overwhelming when the winds of change are blowing. For me, being around my family gave me enough of the familiar to calm the troubled waters. I was young and insecure, and my ability to empathize with my wife was nonexistent. I took her wanting to leave very personally, like it was all about me. It's staggering that I couldn't see just a few of these realities. I would allow something that had nothing to do with me affect our relationship for years to come.

It was a challenging year – what with moving into our own apartment, a new school, my wife's job as a receptionist, and, of course, the arrival of a little girl. We were broke, with barely enough to feed ourselves, in addition to having a newborn to care for. We really didn't know each other very well, yet here we were married, having a daughter together. It seemed almost surreal. On top of everything we were juggling, the tension at home was sometimes unbearable. The level of frustration for me would cause me to run: I would get in my car and leave, sometimes only for ten minutes, other times for hours. During one of our worst fights, my anger spilled over to such a violent outburst that I kicked a large hole in the wall and punched the door as hard as I could. After this particular outburst I left. The days that followed haunted me: every time I saw the damage I had caused, I would cringe to myself. What was wrong with me? This wasn't normal behavior. This level of violence and loss of control frightened me. What made it worse was I had no clue where the anger was coming from. My father had told me over the years that I had a big chip on my shoulder. I thought, maybe the two are connected somehow. My wife and I would sweep it under the rug, without any discussion. The embarrassment of my behavior made that easy to do. In fact, though I am no handyman, I learned really fast how to patch the sheetrock, and surprisingly I did a pretty good job.

Our daughter arrived without complication – everything went beautifully. I almost passed out in the delivery room. I looked at myself in the mirror: I was shocked to see that my face was much paler than my poor wife's. Our little girl looked like she had been in a fist-fight. One ear was smashed, her nose was mashed – she looked like she had been through a battle. Of course we were delighted and proud. We had agreed on the name Maryn. Our first daughter, she would give us joy, frustration, laughter, despair, loss of sleep and many smiles. We adored her, as every parent rightly does.

Every Mormon family traditionally has their baby blessed in church on fast and testimony day. If you are in good standing with the church the father usually performs the blessing. This is a big day: the blessing is to record the baby's name officially with the church, the beginning of a process where you are not let go of easily. It would be the last baby blessing I would participate in. I was really active in all my church duties, teaching five- and six-year-olds in the primary, attending all my church meetings, on a timeline that I wasn't fully aware of. My yearning to break free of the tribe was slowly returning. The rebel in me would serve as the catalyst for my departure. I continued to attend church meetings, and wondered what the hell I was doing there. I was frustrated, and feeling once again the isolation I desperately needed – the space to be, whatever having space meant. I would slowly find out.

I was now in chiropractic school studying around the clock. I had a beautiful little girl, and a wife who was no longer working. We were living on student loans and barely scraping by. It was very challenging, to say the least; but we made the best of it. There were a couple of Mormon students in my class whom I befriended in the beginning, but I found myself drifting in the direction of the non-Mormons – their authenticity and acceptance caused an inner struggle as to what side I would choose. Here was exactly the problem I could see: what the hell were we picking sides for? The divisive nature of my beliefs was rearing its head again. For the first time I was becoming acutely aware of this terrible truth about my own religion.

My first year of school opened my mind to the idea that physical healing happened from the inside, not externally. This made perfect sense to me. How else was the body going to heal? It can only heal from the inside, through an intelligence that is far greater than the mind. This inside-out philosophy spilled over into my religious beliefs too: the pieces didn't seem to fit anymore. This doorway to my consciousness opened only a sliver; the light on the other side wasn't yet visible.

Our darling little Maryn was eighteen months old, and we were once again expecting at the end of the year. We were filled with excitement and anticipation. Life was moving at a crazy pace, between school and all my studying. It seemed like I was never home, and when I was home I was studying. Getting to know the woman I was married to never seemed to be a priority; unfortunately, in our culture, 'the cart before the horse' certainly applied: getting to know each other would have to wait. We would get to it one day, I thought. Our casual attitude towards nurturing and growing our relationship would eventually come full circle; but for the time being it was put your seatbelt on. Life would continue to squeeze all it could out of me, as long as I wanted to remain just a spectator.

In July of 1999, only three months before our second child was due to arrive, I decided it was time for a sabbatical from my religion. My sabbatical began at a weekend chiropractic seminar in 'sin city', Las Vegas. I was back drinking and partying like I would never get the chance to again. We had a great time, and it felt like a good release for me. Flying home, I had time for some quiet reflection and feelings of guilt at letting everyone down. I had strayed slightly from the Mormon path before – what was the big deal? I didn't break any laws. Nevertheless I felt like I was a small child again, having to explain why I wasn't home at a certain time. It was a big risk for me to take – I had no idea if my wife would pack up and head home – but it was obviously a risk I was willing to take. If I could have looked into a crystal ball and seen the future I would have second-guessed everything; the immaturity of my soul would have retreated due to the amount of guilt my upbringing taught me to carry. The path I took would forever change my life. How I would be treated by my culture, family and friends would leave me in a state of disbelief.

The divisive nature of the Mormons' beliefs – our path is for everyone, our truth should be your truth – often leaves behind a long list of casualties. In the months ahead I was subjected to criticism from family members and so-called friends. The first confrontations came from the few Mormon 'friends' I associated with at school, and led to them never speaking to me again. That was to be expected; I saw that one coming. I was leveled, though, when I learned from my wife that my parents encouraged her to leave me. Pack up and leave him, they told her: this might scare him enough to come back to the church. I should have seen that one coming too, but you simply don't want to believe that attacks will come so close to home. My wife decided to stick it out for the time being; perhaps I would come around eventually.

My mindset was one of rebellion and freedom: I longed to be left alone, without actually being alone. I was now fully engaged in crossing the barrier between cultural boundaries. I had signed up for the rite of passage only to learn that the passage was far from safe. For the most part my journey began with a middle finger aimed at the Mormons: like it or dislike it, I am moving towards a path that is unfamiliar and scary. I had no direction, no compass, no reference, so therefore I kicked and screamed like a child. I could always come back – and their love would return, wouldn't it? I was rejected for now, but the fact that I may return to the heavenly fold must carry some weight. It was only the beginning of my departure from their truth; surely one day I could return with humility and sorrow. The amount of guilt created so much frustration, guilt that continued to grow within me. This I would smother with more defiance and shame. Once again I hid behind my middle finger and take-no-prisoner style of play. I was lacking self-esteem, therefore I used anger and rage to cover this void. My footing was slippery; I suffered the climber's fear of tumbling over the icy cliff into the unknown. .

Our dear little Chloe was born: she was beautiful and fragile. She seemed to arrive with a still presence, so different from her older sister, yet perfect in all her beauty. I was absent for the first few months of her life, studying for exams. It seemed like it was all a blur. My wife was amazing – she cared for two small children with very little support, and I was thankful although I took it mostly for granted. I was playing so many different roles, and this left very little room for me to be an honest observer of others. For the time being my role was carefully acted out: I was optimistic, carefree and chauvinistic. Women were second-class citizens, weren't they? Certainly they were in my immediate family – my sisters always seemed to be an afterthought. Culturally speaking, within the church, women really don't have a voice. I had previously been following certain religious boundaries, and this proved the perfect recipe for control: stay within the priesthood circle and your wife and children become your little flock, and you their shepherd. Revelation from God on behalf of your family comes through a male priesthood holder, but only if he strictly adheres to the teachings of Mormon doctrine. I was straying from this role so I was losing inspirational leadership for my family, and also any support from male leaders in the church.

I had come to a point in my life where I had had enough – I really didn't care. Or maybe I did care at some level; I just hid it really well. Leaving a culture and doctrine such as the Mormon Church doesn't happen overnight. It is different for everyone, of course it is; for me it would be ten long years before I would fully cut the cords that had held me prisoner for so long. Even discontinuing church attendance put me in the category of the 'less active' – the Mormon term for a member who no longer shows up for church. A small army moves around the periphery of your life trying to get you back into the fold. They really believe they are motivated through love and concern. From their perspective if they don't get you back to church, you will be cast out of heaven forever, never to see your loved ones again. The devil has power over your life, all spirit has been removed. It is extremely heavy baggage. My initial attitude early in my absence was, don't worry, I will eventually come back. I genuinely believed at the time that this was all true. The devil must be in me; I just didn't give a shit about it.

At this stage, my wife was advised by family and friends on numerous occasions to leave me immediately. The pressure must have been very difficult for her, and it took its toll on our fragile relationship. Now, with two small children, the way backward seemed impossible, and we both felt compelled to keep it all together. The underlying hope from family was that the prodigal son would return when he came to his senses. This belief would only buy me so much time. If there was any real direction I had, it was finishing school – as long as I could maintain average grades and graduate, I would be fine. The geographical distance from our cultural upbringing in Utah certainly gave me enough space to take the first step on my personal journey away from the church – perhaps I would have caved after the withdrawal of conditional love from family, if we had been living in Utah.

Chapter 11

Graduation to Career

I was now a little over the halfway mark to graduating from chiropractic school. We desperately needed extra money – my student loans would only take us so far each semester, and feeding four mouths was a constant struggle. Occasionally when my in-laws were in town, they would fill our cupboards with food. I was really thankful for this – it was a kind gesture when we were in a tough spot. My father-in-law had the ability to be generous; but unfortunately, as with many Mormons, the generosity comes with very heavy strings attached, and in his case it was no different. I found a job valet-parking cars at a nightclub on the weekends. It was tough staying out until three in the morning, but it was a good job that brought additional income, and we could now buy plenty of food. This was a huge relief; before I found the job, our cupboards were almost completely empty. It was a big sacrifice, though, to be gone as much as I was – I missed a lot in my girls' lives. Of course my relationship with my wife continued to suffer. We weren't fighting a whole lot anymore – we simply weren't around each other enough to ever have a fight.

One of my brothers graduated and headed back home to Utah with his small family. Eight months later my oldest brother also graduated and returned to Utah. With my father's help and financial backing, a small family practice was established. It was a shaky start, but to their credit they managed to stay afloat.

We were still back in Texas, where I was finishing school. We had already been joined by two of my younger sisters and their husbands - it seemed that the call to chiropractic school traveled through our family. Seeking an individual path eluded a few of us; it certainly had eluded me. Taking ownership and responsibility for my decisions had been well out of reach. I had followed a path and teaching that was not my own. Stepping out on my own would expose every aspect of myself, and the fear of overexposure was keeping me paralyzed, trapped in the very chains I held the key to.

The last year we spent in Texas would turn out to be pivotal in the later development of my life path. I created a network of friends, all of whom sincerely accepted me for who I was. Between my jobs – valet-parking and a Sunday afternoon golf-club job – my network slowly grew. I began to have fun. Taking life a little less seriously felt good. But from my family's perspective I was now spiraling out of control. My wife tried to support me, but her perspective was the same as our families'.

The truth was that my life *was* spinning out of control – I was far from being anchored or grounded. Perhaps the most important ingredient in gaining control of your life is to experience its opposite, to watch your life spin out of control, turning you completely on your ass. The perspective gained from viewing both sides of the coin is worth the pain and suffering. It's what I like to call experience – the most painful teacher, but god do you learn. When loved ones try to shelter us from the harsh experiences and lessons of life they potentially cripple our creative connection with life itself. The freedom to experience life in all its beauty and harshness should be as important as every man, woman and child's right to breathe.

My ever-growing connections in the city helped my chiropractic skills. I sometimes would have a line of people waiting to receive an adjustment. I was more than willing to reciprocate: their need for a little relief, my need to practice on live bodies. It worked out so well the owners of the club wanted to set me up in a building of my own after I graduated. I was blown away with the offer – what a wonderful compliment, if nothing else. They believed in me. Wow, having someone believe in me felt amazing.

My wife, on the other hand, didn't share my enthusiasm – to put it mildly. In fact the whole idea of staying in Texas and not returning to Utah scared her. The fact that I had discontinued attending church meant I was now a wide-open target: whatever had gone wrong or could go wrong, it would all be my fault. My leaving the church left her feeling vulnerable, isolated; I couldn't be completely trusted anymore. The divisive nature of this religion leaves very little wiggle room, especially inside a marriage that is literally sanctioned by the church. The conditioned culture we had both been raised in put her in a very difficult position, one that at times I couldn't possibly see. The stark difference between our individual realities would remain in the dark for now. Fear would keep the door closed to the possibility of a whole new light. Connecting the dots was something I was not well versed in.

Returning to Utah with the prodigal son was the outcome my wife had hoped for. She made a few phone calls to her father, looking for an intervention to thwart any further plans to stay and build a new practice in Texas. I learned of those phone calls a few years later. It bothered me that my wife had done this behind my back. I felt that it was an act of betrayal, going to her father before her husband. I was far too insecure to listen to my inner voice when it whispered a new path for me and our little family. At the time I did not know exactly what it was that I wanted for myself. The time had not arrived where I could take responsibility for my own choices.

Graduation finally arrived: it was exciting yet surreal. Our two little girls were now three and a half and eighteen months old. We were on our way back to the nest, Utah, to join the family practice, take our place at the family table. It was no one's fault. It was my decision – I simply wasn't ready to accept the unknown, and the comfort of the known was still safe, for now. It was hard for me to leave my small network of friends in Texas who had accepted me for who I was. They threw me a small going-away party – these people who would be reviled in my culture. It was done with real, unconditional love. I had been a valet, for godsakes, what did I have to offer other than my friendship? It was a lesson I dearly needed to learn, one of many lessons that further down the road would bring a little comfort.

It has always been my experience that conditional love, in all its stringy attachment, seems to come from those who belong to rigid belief systems. Their capacity to radiate the energy of love in its unconditional state – the only state true love dwells in – seems so far out of reach, because their narrow view of truth isolates, divides, conquers. It seems that society has been far more comfortable with conflict and violence than the pure energy of love. Being right, or holding a banner of truth, has unfortunately outweighed the true beauty of love.

We arrived in Utah with the help of my parents – they towed all our belongings back home. We stayed in the basement of my parents' house, while my oldest brother occupied a small apartment on my parents' property. In the event, my small family would last only two weeks with my parents. I received my final and very rewarding passing score from my board examinations – a crucial step in becoming licenced in the state of Utah. My family all went to dinner to celebrate my success. Afterwards my oldest brother and I went to celebrate with a few drinks. My father's control issues were far from gone: it was like he rolled back time, and we were teenagers again. After our night of celebration, the next day my father told me, my wife and small family to move out. Go and find somewhere else to live. My oldest brother and his family would remain in my parents' apartment. It seemed that my father's fear still had a firm grip on control, especially when it came to his children. He still took it all so personally when his children behaved differently than him. Would my father's insecurities ever allow him to let go of control?

My in-laws took us in immediately, and we lived with them for a couple of months. I was twenty-eight years old, in a brand-new career that I was really excited about. I will never forget the events that unfolded during this period of my life. I was licensed in July, building my own clientele alongside my older brothers. They had made enough room for me in their small practice. A third of the office overhead was my responsibility, and I also inherited a forty-thousand-dollar debt that I was expected to pay back. At the time I was happy to have a familiar place to safely land at the start of my new career.

I awoke one morning and witnessed, with the rest of the country, the shock and horror of 9/11. I left for work that morning feeling different, somehow empty. I couldn't help thinking that the culture that gave birth to those horrors I had witnessed on television was the direct result of religious fanaticism. This took me right back to my own culture. I was living it – certainly not on the level of the atrocities of 9/11, but wasn't it the same divisive energy that allows people to justify such acts of violence and horror? It was a thought I couldn't shake.

We moved into our first home in the beginning of 2002. We were excited and proud to be new homeowners, our first real step in laying down some shaky roots. My small business grew a little each day, and this gave us some breathing room, with just enough to pay the bills and a little money left over. I had a brief moment to enjoy some accomplishment and success. It was a relatively peaceful year in our marriage; there was still conflict, but financial success helped ease some of the tension. I hadn't yet completely ruled out going back to the church – it was still a real possibility from my family's perspective, and from mine as well. My wife was attending church functions and taking the children along. The pressure that slowly followed was natural, due to the fact that we had moved right into the thick of Mormon culture. Deflecting the pressure to return to the fold only lasted so long, and the tension it caused would eventually almost end our marriage. My drinking on the weekends slowly began to escalate – it was my way of numbing myself to the wounds of abuse – simply put, to the pain of a broken heart.

Chapter 12
Year of Lessons

We were once again expecting a little girl, due early the following year. During the pregnancy our relationship continued to suffer. Spending any time around my in-laws was excruciatingly uncomfortable – the tension was palpable, along with the contempt I felt from them and from my own family. It became a burden I no longer wanted to carry. I got to a point where I gave up caring. My arrogance asserted itself in a combative way that pushed against both families. This continued to chip away at our marriage, alienating my wife and creating more tension. I closed myself off to any kind of resolution. I was working four days a week making a decent living, drinking too much, numbed to the reality of my crumbling marriage. I was floating in a foggy haze of pain, anger and resentment – not a good combination for making sound decisions. Ironically the one thing that was grounding me was exercise – running and biking. The running I had despised in my youth I had taken up again, and it gave some solace to my battered opinion of myself, and would prove over the years ahead to be a solid anchor. The year finished with a two-hundred-mile bike race that I did not finish on account of two flat tires. I abandoned the race feeling somewhat defeated, but promised myself that I would finish the race the following year.

The lessons I needed to learn in 2003 were extremely daunting. They of course served a specific purpose. I had unconsciously signed up to them, creating each one myself. The path that these lessons would put me on would change my life forever: I would never be the same and I would never look back again.

Our little angel Sophie was born the day before my birthday. She was beautiful and full of life, I was proud to be her father. However at the time I was detached from my wife, and especially from her family. My in-laws were certainly good at going through the motions – from the perfect Christmases to gifts at birthdays, they were overachievers. When it came to making a simple connection on a human level, though, the vacancy was blown wide open. They struggled to genuinely connect with anyone. The natural flow of a conversation became strained and proved too difficult. I eagerly sought any excuse to skip out on my wife's family gatherings. Their apparent rejection of who I was returned, with a very passive–aggressive style of play: they would never tell me their true feelings, but the underlying contempt was there. My insecurity only added fuel to their quiet fire.

Lesson number one that year had been slowly building. Two and half months after Sophie was born, I packed up and left: I wanted a divorce. I had a three-month affair that I kept secret, hoping that my wife would make the choice to divorce me. I was not only lying to my wife, I was lying to myself, gutless to make a decision because of the fear of what family and friends might think of me. My wife suspected a girlfriend, and her accusations were spot on. My initial guilt masqueraded in the form of anger and denial. I was still afraid to step up and take ownership of my choices. After two weeks of a hell that I created, I returned home with even more chauvinistic bravado. My ego was far from finished asserting itself into my life; in fact it was running my life. My expectations for our future, if we both remained in the marriage, were laid out on the table. No religion, no more pressure, I told my wife: if we can proceed in this way, I'm in; if not, I'm out. My intolerance for this religion that I now held responsible for all my problems was no longer going to control my life.

My bravado only worked for so long. The underlying guilt that I had desperately tried to suffocate would be directly responsible for a new journey that I was about to embark on. My insensitivity and my use of control in trying to rewire our marriage would come full circle.

For the time being we forged ahead, spending little or no time discussing the details of our near collapse. In my short absence her mother had stepped in to clean our home, take care of the kids and get my wife placed on anti-depressants. The Mormon population in Utah have one of the highest rates in the US of women and children in drug therapy for depression. I managed a confession to my wife that I had an affair. I was pulled over after two pitchers of beer and received a citation for intoxication. My truck was impounded and I had to attend a week of nightly classes, not to mention a one-thousand-dollar fine. Spiraling out of control would be a spot-on way to describe what was happening. Lesson number two was quickly digested.

We were back together, standing on a foundation that had been cracked wide open. My wife agreed to back away from the church; all activities with the church stopped. My wife got her first taste of rejection – her family sent her emails telling her to come back, and then communication with her parents came to a standstill. The silent but deadly control was in full swing. They hated the fact that their daughter was putting her marriage before the church. Their withdrawal from their daughter's life was so obvious to me that I observed it with disdain. It was the same control and rejection I had received from my family, just much more elusive. Not saying a word to the person you are rejecting makes it so much more difficult for the rejected person to be aware that it is happening. On top of this, the last thing you want to believe is that your own family is rejecting you. It is a very difficult pill to swallow, especially when you believe your family is perfect. The rejection I received from my family was in your face; her family's rejection was silent and unannounced. Now that I was stepping back from my cultural conditioning, it was obvious to me what was going on.

Facing the full swing of Mormon rejection is not for the faint-hearted. It comes in a few stages. The first stage is shame and guilt – we love you but we have to withdraw some of our love, slightly alienate you. The next stage comes only if you are still out of the church, however this is where it gets tricky. If you are a fence-sitter, meaning you still halfway believe in the church being true, they will mildly stay with you, give you some support. In the third stage, once you take a personal stand that you no longer believe in the church, you have committed family and social suicide: they will treat you like a traitor. The niceties that follow come with a thick layer of insincerity and the disdain towards you is palpable.

The guilt I was wrestling with over my affair, along with my bitterness and frustration, caused enough suffering that I desperately needed an outlet. I turned once again to pedaling my bike. I spent a few months logging close to two thousand miles on my bike. It was therapy, my escape from the insanity of my culture and myself. I entered the two-hundred-mile bike race again, and managed to finish in a respectable time. I was proud of finishing something I had set out to do. It was a small accomplishment, but a very rewarding one. It was the last bike race I entered: my heart wasn't really in it.

Soon after the bike race my family went to my parents' for a Halloween gathering. After a few drinks, I was wrestling with my younger brother, who outweighed me in size and strength. It was friendly brotherly playfulness – we were both laughing. But then my left foot got caught somehow and turned cleanly inwards, almost all the way around. Everyone heard the snap: it was sickening to hear. My foot was literally flopping at the end of my leg. I was carried to the car, and my wife and brother took me to the hospital. I was in shock. The alcohol helped dull the pain – I didn't really feel anything. I later learned that my fibula had broken clean through, right at the bottom of my leg, and a couple of ligaments in my ankle had torn right off the bone. I was in surgery the next morning. When we left the hospital that evening I was in a cast up to my knee, with six screws and a plate. Finishing off the year this way left me wondering if perhaps this was karma. My actions leading up to my broken ankle were thoughtless and out of control. It gave me time to reflect on the pain I had caused my wife. Lesson number three that year: don't drink and wrestle your brother who is much bigger and stronger. This also closed the chapter of the first four years since I had discontinued attending church activities. It was time to find myself, whoever that might be.

The path I was about to embark on would mark for me the beginning of my spiritual journey. At the time I had no idea that this was the direction I was headed in. I no longer had any intention of returning to the Mormons; they had already shared their version of love, and I wanted no part in that. Unfortunately, though, that part was far from over. The fact that they believe they are the only religion on the planet that has all truth only blinds them to the division it causes. Their blind faith in salvation in the next life seems to allow them to justify their behavior in the here and now. My wife and I were still on shaky ground: recovering from such a blow is hard enough when you are on the same page with your beliefs. The fact that we were no longer seeing anything eye to eye made it almost impossible to heal and move on.

I miraculously found myself in my own office in the beginning of 2004. To my surprise, one brother went further south and the other brother left the country. I had no idea then that it would be the last time I would work in the same office with my brothers. We had of course had good times and bad times working together; we were three completely different personalities. I was happy to be on my own for the first time since graduation. I was eager to move from our community, which was heavily populated with Mormons; there were some neighbors who wouldn't even wave to me. It was awkward and strange to be treated like I somehow wasn't human. The rejection gets heavy, it can wear you down; many go back to the church because of that heavy feeling of rejection. Moving to a different community was an option, one we definitely looked at, but the opportunity didn't present itself for the time being.

I made the decision to join with a chiropractic managing company. Their home base was in New York, but they had seminars all over the country. The company blended chiropractic along with personal development, with a heavier emphasis on personal development. It was, surprisingly, a welcoming atmosphere – one that I was unfamiliar with. The goal was for people to become a better version of themselves through this approach, and to expand their life and their business. A personal coach was assigned to each person, they had one phone call with their coach each week, and attended five seminars a year. It was a new experience for me, one that would finally steer me in the right direction. I was introduced to a whole new world of fantastic speakers and books. It was a great place for me to land. Finally I had some purpose and direction outside organized religion.

When I first attended one of their seminars I felt awkward, uncomfortable, and I still had a thick layer of arrogance. I was like, 'I'm fine, I don't need to work on myself.' At a much deeper level, though, I knew that I was far from being at peace with myself. The truth was I was afraid to really examine myself closely. I slowly began to see that I was a scared little boy. This would take years to fully admit; but for now, I was tentatively on the path to personal examination and I wasn't getting off, not after all I had been through. I was in, I couldn't go backwards. It was one foot in front of the other.

The next four and a half years were full of struggle and dogged determination, self-rejection and lack of faith inwardly. Believe me, many times I wanted to abandon what seemed like a hopeless journey; but I couldn't give up on myself. I was in search of the truth. I now knew the truth couldn't be in my childhood-taught doctrines that were based on a culture set on control and fear and with a history of burying the truth. The mechanics of that whole rigid structure self-destructed the moment I looked within.

I read like never before. I had read all the Mormon books; now it was time to study books that offered a much different perspective. I devoured every book I could get my hands on. We were now doing well enough financially – my little practice was expanding, though not by any huge standard. My attitude was overly optimistic, filled with emptiness, lacking in substance. I wasn't well grounded: my energy was large but it was all over the place, scattered.

My resistance towards my Mormon family was seen by them as bitterness and anger. That had been my past, yet they could not let the labels about me go. I figured, if you get to speak your mind about your beliefs, then so do I. What I was about to learn would take some time. In Utah, the Mormon culture hasn't been challenged, certainly not on an individual level. They are not used to being questioned: they are the only ones who are supposed to ask the questions so, naturally, turning the tables on their home turf stirs up emotions. It became apparent that if you offend a Mormon, the backlash is not pleasant. I felt that, for the time being, I could handle the negative energy. At least now with my in-laws it was on the table for all to see, I could now touch it, put my finger on their negativity. Beforehand, the negative energy of their rejection had been hidden; in a passive culture like Utah's, where the energy is very repressive, it can be difficult to identify.

My wife and I continued looking for a new place to move to. We centered on the community that my parents lived in, and my wife's parents lived just a twenty-minute drive away. Spreading our wings had apparently never occurred to us. Our sights were set on staying close to what we were familiar with – or rather what I was familiar with. All I could see was moving to the little mountain community where I had spent the bulk of my childhood. My new journey had happened; I would slow it down by keeping what was comfortable close.

After months of looking we found what we believed was the perfect spot, a piece of land that we could build on. We managed to acquire a loan for the land, and we were able to make payments towards our little piece of real estate. I was so excited to move, I could almost taste it. Our new plan became, for me, my future salvation from my unhappy self. I saw this move as an escape from the insanity of our culture. In reality this was only a lateral move, but I saw it as a step in the right direction. Perhaps in some ways it was: moving closer to my family would artificially allow me to feel safe.

But it wouldn't last long. I was now almost thirty-one years old. My father had never even acknowledged the abuse – it was expected that it would be forgotten. The word abuse was never used to define anything in my youth, nor would it ever be used by my parents. I didn't believe it myself: everything I remembered about my childhood I would laugh at, if I even acknowledged that certain things had happened. My laughter was a mask I had hidden behind for years. The pain that emerged as anger and bitterness wanted badly to heal, but it was far too covered up, too deep, far out of reach from the loving embrace that healing promised. Laughter would only work for so long. At the time I was a master at showing myself how whole I was as a human being. I think I may have been the only one convinced that this was even possible. I was hiding from the terrible trauma of abuse. My father, too, had done the same thing and was continuing to do so. His ability to run and hide from the truth was handed down to me – generational running and hiding. There was no blame whatsoever, just the unconscious attempt not to feel the pain of abuse. My father's theme for all my adult years was 'Your mother and I will only remember the good times and forget all the bad.' I heard this over and over again: 'Focus on just the positive', he would say. It almost made me feel bad for bringing up anything from the past that had to do with my abuse.

What I didn't know then, but I know now, is that my father's inability to acknowledge any abuse was continuing to re-subject me to abuse, and so the pattern of abuse remained firmly imprinted in our DNA. I no longer wanted to carry this weight around – it was a bigger burden than I cared to carry. I had to end this cycle of suffering. My challenge was daunting, with very few answers and very little help, but the answers came, one foot in front of the other. I couldn't abandon my call to accept the truth, not now, after all these years. The changes within were painfully slow, and at times my dysfunction and lack of control were on full display. Of course it was during these times that I would judge myself harshly – more harshly than anyone else.

Chapter 13

Taking a Stand against Zion

I had now been with the same managing company for a little over one year. I learned a lot, read some great books. Yet I was frustrated because the change within was minuscule. If there was any change at all, it was that I had gained a small amount of awareness, for the first time in my life, that I needed help.

We decided it was time to sell our house and start construction on our dream home. Moving forward with such lofty goals was scary, especially in light of the amount of debt I had managed to acquire in the short span of two years. I thought we needed to own everything – cars, boats, motorcycles, electronics; my eyes were much bigger than my pocket. My bullshit optimism, which I really believed was an asset, would continue running my life, spinning my financial life out of control. Optimism on its own is beautiful, but mine was layered behind too many masks, its misdirection guided by my trumped-up version of me.

Our house sold relatively quickly, so our small family moved to a condo that we rented for almost a year. It was very close to our soon-to-be home. We felt that everything was where it needed to be. Of course my biggest concern was our marriage. I knew that things hadn't really improved. It seemed to me that our ability to relate to each other had always been missing, and wasn't showing up anytime soon. We felt, though, that continuing our relationship was best for everyone else. Perhaps our new home would help to improve our struggling marriage. My wife had returned to church with our children, and was now regularly attending most church functions. The pressure from her family not only worked really well, it was now denied: it had never existed. I was speechless that my wife would deny something that was so obvious – walking your parents' path is not something most adult children like to admit. Denial of certain facts, culturally speaking, is very common, because of the repressive nature of relationships. Observing a genuine relationship within this culture is rare, especially between parents and their children.

One of the definitions of bigotry is intolerance towards someone else's beliefs. Obviously this can go both ways, and it most certainly did in my life. In the face of their rejection and intolerance of me, I allowed intolerance to rise in myself and directed that energy towards their religious beliefs. I was once again fighting a losing battle. My wife constantly found herself stuck in the middle of this conflict. We both had been taught that the church should be put first at all cost, even if it might cost you your marriage or your physical life. Inviting the long arm of rejection into her life was something she wanted no part of. Seeing it firsthand in my life seemed to be all it took for her to retreat to the familiar. For reasons already stated and some that I perhaps overlooked, she would remain a follower of Mormon beliefs.

I supported my wife the only way I knew how at that time in my life – with indifference and sarcastic humor. As she gently settled back into the fold with the children, my resistance was on full display. I'm sure it was an overreaction to the pressure I got a couple of years earlier. This was a recipe for disaster that would frequently derail our fragile relationship. We were like two frightened children scrambling for security – hers the familiar, mine a journey into the unknown. I was ready to let go personally but I was not ready to let go of my marriage and, most of all, not my children. I felt that I had to stay and fight for them. The only chance my children had of gaining a different perspective was through me. They were growing up fully immersed in the repressive culture. How could I limit the damage that I saw coming? If my children chose the Mormon path, then fine. If they chose a path that was one of their own, I wanted to be there to help them through the rejection. I would make sure that I was there with open arms, allowing them to be whatever they wanted to be.

Our house was now well under construction, and tension between my wife and me was at an all-time high. Verbal was my favorite form of abuse, and escalating to name-calling was not uncommon. The pain and fear from my childhood added more guilt and shame that I was failing at my marriage. I just wanted to succeed at something, distance myself from looking bad – because that was all I believed I was.

I was ashamed of being abused, so I tried to hide behind a tough exterior. My frustration found its release in the form of blame. Blaming others allowed myself to become a victim, and that justified never looking in the mirror at myself. The truth was still too painful to look at directly. Blaming others opened up my right to feel more resentment, and pushed away personal responsibility. Feeling angry pushed away any chance of accessing the spirit of healing. This spiritual energy was not something I was familiar with at this stage in my life. Knowing anything about healing in my emotional world was further down my path. Becoming aware of the fact that I was sick emotionally and needed healing was like glimpsing a small glowing light that hovers over the horizon at dawn. When I first realized this, it scared the hell out of me. I naïvely stepped up to the challenge. I was in fact in desperate need of an emotional physician.

My wife and I began seeing a counselor together. I went reluctantly, with just enough openness to receive some outside help. When I learned that he was a Mormon, that gave me pause, yet I moved forward – with some apprehension. It turned out to be quite helpful. He helped us with our styles of communication, and after a few sessions we enjoyed a relatively peaceful period in our lives. Any tension that remained we chalked up to stress from the construction of our new home, and from our difficult living quarters in the condo, where there was not much room for a family of five. But the underlying stress was really minuscule compared to the real issues. The main issue was, and always would be, that I wasn't going to church. Understand that the church can never be blamed for anything, especially if you are an active Mormon. The last thing you would ever do is place responsibility on the church. The careful prescription over the Mormon-sanctioned marriage means that walking away from the church when you're married is really difficult. If you walk away together, your chances of staying together are obviously much better. In our case, my wife wanted to remain in the church, and the doctrine placed her in a difficult position. She could not get to the Mormon heaven without me, so her world was heavily divided. In essence, if you are not together in the church you are screwed in the next life. This put my wife in an impossible situation. The church, by holding on to this doctrine, creates so much unnatural pressure: either you're all in together or you're all out, there is no middle road.

Our oldest daughter turned eight at the end of the year. It was time for her baptism. I wasn't at all happy about it; she was too young to decide on a religion. But it was not a battle I chose to fight. Of course my father and father-in-law would perform the baptism and confirmation. It was interesting watching two people who couldn't stand the sight of each other, act as though they liked each other. The rigid, unnatural communication between them was hard to watch, especially at my daughter's baptism. It was fascinating, in a way, to observe the tension between two individuals who were essentially on the same team, but who were both big egos that needed to be in control. I often imagined what would have happened had they not shared the same beliefs.

So now my first daughter was a Mormon at the tender age of eight, just like her father and mother. It surely wasn't by choice – what eight-year-old is ready to decide on their religion? They can't possibly know what religion they want to be a part of – if any at all.

Construction of our house was almost complete, and we were excited about moving in to our new home. On the other hand I was stricken with fear that I had taken on too big of a house payment. In truth, I had – not to mention financially pinning myself to my shaky marriage. Leaving little wiggle room within my marriage gave me a false sense of security. I couldn't imagine leaving my children; the thought of them not being in my life was not an option. Ironically I felt somewhat trapped, yet here I was creating more of the same in my own life. As human beings we really love to suffer. We don't think we do, but we create so much suffering for ourselves and of course those around us. It's as though we need it to survive, like it's food. Feeling like I deserved anything other than suffering had eluded me.

I was getting back in to running. The recovery from my injury was slow and painful; and even more so on an emotional level. Hindsight can be extremely helpful. After I broke my ankle I immediately put on twenty-five pounds, and I went through a period of depression. Not having the element of physical release in my life affected me in this way. My emotional world was fragile and delicate, balancing between my unhappy self and my clever patterns of behavior. The additional weight I had put on seemed to complement the emotional baggage I had been carrying most of my life. The two together would comfortably keep me trapped in my little world where I could suffer.

The children were as lively as ever. The two oldest were in school full-time, and our youngest, Sophie, was three and half. From the outside we appeared to be a happy little family, although my wife and I both knew this was not the case. Tension between us returned – it was like it had never left – and divorce was regularly threatened. If I attended family functions with her, it was usually kicking and screaming; most of them I skipped out on. Eventually my wife stopped caring whether I was there or not – in fact, it was easier for her when I wasn't there. She had made her choice – stay with the familiar – and I certainly wasn't going to blame her for that.

The time finally arrived to move into our beautiful new home. The neighborhood was nice, there was even a little diversity; compared to our last community, it was night and day. The girls loved their new school, they had friends to play with. I was happy with my career, my practice was doing well. Everything fit really well – it was almost perfect. My wife and I, though, were making no progress at all. We went back to the same counselor we had used earlier, but we only lasted two sessions. Our last session did not sit well with me – I felt that it was no longer a safe place for me to express myself freely. I told my wife that I could no longer see a Mormon counselor, as their inability to stay neutral and to step beyond the structured walls of their beliefs meant open and free discussion was not possible.

It was around this time in our lives that my wife contemplated a divorce. She spoke to me about it on a couple of occasions. I remember feeling scared and unsure of what might happen. My biggest fear was not having the kids in my life on a daily basis. I was also anxious that it might lead to financial collapse. The possible outcomes were too overwhelming to contemplate, and I was unable to view divorce as a rational solution to our problems. We would have to stay in our marriage. And so we continued our fragile existence.

Moving into our new home created the perfect distraction, temporarily at least, from the real issues. It quickly became the gathering spot for my family, and most family functions were held there. I loved having company over, it didn't matter who it was; anyone who distracted me from myself and my marriage was welcomed with open arms. When I was alone with myself, my thoughts would consume me. My world was turned upside down, and the worrying was killing me. It felt like everyone and everything was unsafe, nothing and no one could be trusted. I had lost my old identity and quickly found a new one. One set of beliefs and ideas had been replaced by another set of beliefs. This clearly was not working for me anymore. I continued reading and searching outside of myself to find peace – perhaps a book that could help me relate to what I was feeling inside – but unfortunately my search was in vain. I felt lost over and over again. The void was large, but I maintained hope that something would find me or I would find it. .

One particular Sunday afternoon my wife and I went to her parents' house for dinner. It had been a few months since my last visit. I generally tried to arrive a little buzzed from a few afternoon cocktails – it helped me to tolerate the uneasy relationship we had. Conversation was usually brief between my father-in-law and me – he would ask me a few basic questions and then forget to listen to the answer. Sometimes I didn't answer at all, to see if he was listening; sure enough he didn't even notice that I hadn't responded. This lack of interest became almost amusing; the vacancy was startling to observe. To my surprise he asked me how I felt about the church. Now understand, I knew I was at a crossroads here. At this point in our marriage their support, I suspected, was shaky but still there. I could proceed in one of two ways. The first option was to tell him I wasn't sure – on the fence so to speak – and leave it at that. If

I wanted to keep their shaky support intact, option one would have been a good decision. I went with option two, at which point I knew there would be no return. I told him exactly how I felt – essentially, I told him I thought the Mormon beliefs were all just a fairytale. I didn't like all the lies I had been told. I also didn't like the changes the church leaders had made over the years, the cover-up of certain facts within church history, the removal of prior taught Mormon doctrine. And I no longer wanted anything to do with their control and rejection. My father-in-law was having a tough time not falling out of his chair. As far as my in-laws were concerned I was literally hammering the last nail in my coffin, and I knew it. Of course he maintained his passive role and tried to be as nice as he could to me. He rarely, if ever, allowed anyone to see that his feathers were ruffled. From that conversation it was only a matter of when his daughter was ready to call it quits; he would immediately come and save her and his granddaughters from the devil himself.

My self-deluded arrogance marched on. I convinced myself that I was once again in control and running my own life. The knowledge I thought I had gained from all the books I had read gave me a security blanket to hide behind. It was my new arsenal, and I would use it to verbally level anyone from the Mormon community who got in my way. The phone rang one evening. On the other end was someone I didn't even know. He said, 'Brother Preston, could we schedule a time for you and your wife to come in for tithing settlement.' I was shocked that they would even call. I was trigger-happy; I responded, 'I don't give a rat fuck about your tithing.' My poor wife immediately snatched the phone out of my hand and apologized on my behalf. Once again I was destroying certain relationships. I was thoughtless and very childish in my behavior. My actions were like those of a defiant adolescent, telling the whole world to go fuck themselves.

My spiritual journey seemed at times to be anything but spiritual. Rather, my anger asserted itself right up front in my life. I was becoming the embodiment of what they wanted me to become. When you leave the church, they want to paint you into one of two corners: either you are angry and bitter, or you are homosexual or lesbian – these are their favorite stereotypes if you have left the fold. If they can't put you in their box, they want you in a box that they believe is abhorred by God. They draw a massive line in the sand: what side of the line are you on is a language they are very fluent in. As in all battles there can never be any conquering hero: everyone loses.

It was now eight years since I had stopped going to any religious services. I was weary and frustrated. I decided it was time to close the chapter of my seminar management company connection. I had learned a lot about myself, and I had met some inspirational authors and spiritual guides. The doorway had been opened for me; eventually I would choose to walk through. I had now been in my career as a chiropractor for six years. I loved my profession and I had a great relationship with some of my patients. My frustration with the ups and downs of running a small business was taking its toll, however. I felt somewhat trapped and isolated within the walls of my small office. I began to feel within myself that I needed to write a book. The thought felt overwhelming and impossible, and besides, what was I going to write about? The notion to write lingered – it appeared to be just a thought in my head, and it would remain just a thought for a couple more years.

A good friend of mine whom I met while working out in the local gym seemed to show up at the right time. The student was ready; the teacher appeared. I badly needed some guidance. He and his wife happened to be ex-Mormons, so our friendship developed with empathy and understanding. We had some good times together. They were further down the road than I, and they helped lift some of my guilt and anger. They gave me a book for my birthday, which I saw as something to devour and move on to the next book. It was like I was always in a hurry. This showed up in every aspect of my life – everyone who knew me, knew that I was impatient and intolerant towards those who made me wait. The book they gave me was *The Power of Now* by Eckhart Tolle. I read it in a few days then, arrogantly, put it down and thought, that was a good read, what can I read next? That book would remain on my bookcase for the next couple of years; thank god it was never thrown away. The teacher always appears when the student is ready: this became my mantra. I was ready to make the important changes that would make a difference, my eyes were open, awaiting a sunrise that beckoned a new day. The fact that I was still holding on to my pain slowed my progress to access a bright new beginning. Feeling safe was my dream – I just did not know how to feel safe. I realized that safety no longer existed with my upbringing, so looking elsewhere was my chosen response. Safety lay in walking my own life path, following what I had always been told to silence – my inner voice.

Chapter 14
Broken Wide Open

It was the winter of 2007–08. It was absolutely incredible, we had so much snow: I remember there being a few days where we had well over twenty inches in one day. Being Utah, the snow was light and fluffy, perfect for snowboarding or skiing. Locals in the area figured we hadn't enjoyed a winter that big since the 1983–84 season. My two older brothers and I were season-pass holders at one of the local resorts. We spent a lot of time together that season, carving up the mountain as much as we could. It was a real joy spending some quality time with my brothers. There had always been a little resentment in our family towards my oldest brother. It really wasn't his fault my father created the dysfunctional dynamics, the way he thought a family should operate, mangled through the lens of abuse, biblical distortion and religious fanaticism.

It was towards the end of the season. We had spent the morning in fresh powder, it was beautiful. We were in the lodge eating some lunch, when tension surfaced between my oldest brother and myself. Before I knew it the tension had risen to full-blown verbal abuse. He completely lost it – name-calling and hitting as close to home as he possibly could. He happened to nail everything spot on, barely missing any detail – my mountain of debt, all the shit I owned but never really owned – he must have gone on for several minutes. I barely got a single word in, I didn't need to: I was speechless. At that moment I absorbed it all. Everything he had said to me stung severely, yet I was content to let it be.

We didn't speak for almost a month after that, but my brother's tirade turned out to be a really good predictor for my life ahead. My finances were out of control. The pressure I put on my small business to outperform my reckless spending had reached its capacity. I was like a sailor looking for the promised land of materialism only to see the expanse of the vast ocean swallow me whole. My ego's identifying with material possessions was coming to an end.

I turned thirty-five that spring; my daughters were ten, eight and five. My wife and I were further apart than ever, and the facade of our happy lives was soon to be blown apart. It was one foot in front of the other, unsure and uncertain as to the events that would unfold. I was scared yet somehow ready for my path to blossom. There was a calm presence for a couple of months – I wasn't aware of it at the time – but the stillness was perhaps me sitting in the eye of a massive storm.

It was Mother's Day 2008. This was one of the few occasions each year I would go to my in-laws for dinner. Ironically, it was one of the few times I remembered to get my wife a gift other than the usual card. My father-in-law seemed somewhat smug, more so than I had ever seen him before. My wife was now on her parents' side, and on this occasion I saw myself as an outsider. It was just a glimpse, and I didn't want to believe it. How long had I been oblivious to something that must have been so obvious? The events that unfolded would prove I wasn't yet ready to let go. I wanted to go home: I needed to get out of there immediately. I told my wife, 'Let's go,' and she replied, 'I'm not ready to leave yet.' I simply said, 'If you're not coming, I'm leaving.' Her response was 'I don't care anymore, leave me here.' I didn't want to leave her and our children there; I had come this far with her family and I was sick of playing a passive role. I wasn't about to retreat. I left with an empty feeling of uncertainty and rejection, along with the sting of betrayal. I had seen it, and her actions were spelling out the truth: the church and her family came well before me. I drove home to an empty house. I was frustrated and angry, yet under it all a scared little boy. My financial meltdown had begun and my marriage was unraveling for the first time with my wife leading the charge.

I hardly slept that night. The next morning I arrived at my office, uncertain of my path that lay ahead. My wife called and told me quite emphatically she wanted a divorce. I was winded and shaky; there was nothing else to say in that phone conversation. I arrived home that evening to a clean house. A good portion of my children's toys and clothes were gone. It seemed as though she was ready to see it through. I felt alone, rejected and betrayed; my insecurity was at an all-time high. What would I do without my children in my life every day? My second identity was slowly shattering: I would be alone. How could I be alone, after eleven years of marriage? It penetrated deep into my empty heart. Over the next few days I leaned heavily on my own family, mostly my parents – I wore them out. I was no longer thinking for myself – had I ever? My insecurity and neediness drove me in the direction of my perception of safety. What I would later learn was that I was nowhere near safety – I had fallen into the arms of control and fear. It wouldn't last long. The whole world was conspiring to give me the opportunity to finally let go. The question was, would I be ready?

The anger and bravado that were thinly masked melted away; I was broken into pieces. Midweek I fell apart emotionally on the phone to my mother. I cried like I had never cried before, my face was wet with giant tears. Ten minutes later I sobbed on my receptionist's shoulder. She hugged me and cried with me. She was a safe, beautiful friend that day. The tears dried up and I felt somewhat better. It was an emotional release I desperately needed.

That Saturday I had a half marathon I was running in, a local race. I asked my wife if she could bring the children to see me at the finish line. As I neared the finish line I cried again. I must have searched every face in the crowd for my children, I looked and looked, to no avail: she hadn't brought them. My parents were there to cheer me on, along with some of my nieces and nephews. It was good to have some support at a time that I really needed it.

My father encouraged me to take a two-week trip to New Zealand, visit some of my family. I was hesitant at first, but after giving it some thought I decided it might just be really good for me. The following week my father found me an inexpensive flight, leaving in ten days. It was a Tuesday evening; the next evening I would book my trip. I was holding off in the hope that my wife would return – I wanted one last talk with her before leaving the country. She agreed to meet me the following morning. I remember pulling into the small isolated parking lot we had arranged to meet at. As soon as I pulled up next to her car she started sobbing uncontrollably. I couldn't hear her, of course, but I sensed immediately that the bravado was gone. What came next shocked the both of us. She had taken a pregnancy test in the public toilet just minutes earlier: she was pregnant. She was devastated, to say the least. I felt a wave of relief; all I could see was getting my children back in my life, and perhaps reclaiming some of my damaged identity. She reluctantly moved back home that day. I suspected the reluctance came from the pressure she would no doubt be getting from her family. The first few days that my wife was home, I received her with open arms. But it was more about me and my neediness than it was about her: I was not ready to fully let go.

My wife explained to me that while she was staying with her family her father called to talk to her three times a day. When she decided to come back to our marriage, the contact from her father ended. This immediate withdrawal from her family left little doubt about the outcome they had hoped for: the demise of our marriage.

I was happy to have my little family back, even though I knew the road ahead would be challenging. I had had some time to reflect over the events of my life. Right in front of me were all the books I had read. One book stood out: I immediately felt an intense desire to reread it. That book was *The Power of Now*, the same book I had read two years earlier. I opened the book, devouring every word. Every sentence was meant for me, it was so clear. Occasionally I would stop reading and lose myself in the moment. I didn't put the book down until I was finished. I became immediately aware that who I thought I was all my life had nothing to do with who I actually was. My fragile state that I had created had allowed everything to melt away. What I saw was myself sitting on cement steps metaphorically observing the person I thought I was in that moment, not a revelation but a slowed down image of me seeing a construct within my own mind. I could now watch myself, it was quite animated with a great deal of relief. The reason it was a relief, was that I was no longer a believer in my old identity – it was just a thought in my head. I had become the watcher of my thoughts, without judgment. A transformation had taken place. Life all of a sudden lost its heaviness. I laughed out loud – it was very funny to me, all those years that I had taken life so seriously. My transformation would unfold like a delicate flower over the next year and a half.

Having the advantage of observing my new state of being gave me a great deal of lightness. Judgment of my thoughts and actions fell away. It was as though I had finally arrived to meet my new friend, life. It was there all along; where the hell had I been? That moment would forever change the way I would see everything and everyone. The shedding of my old self had taken place. I needed time to observe any old pattern that might reassert itself into my life, habits that I was not even aware of. It was my new calling: simple, non-judgmental observation of how my mind and ego had been running my life for thirty-five years. It seemed to return me to my earlier lessons on physical healing in chiropractic school – how that healing happens on the inside first. The full circle of that truth had finally arrived, the truth I had been seeking for five years. It was with me all along. I was truth and beauty the entire time, my very existence radiated love simply by accepting who I was in all my humanness, loving my imperfections with compassion, not judgment.

Soon after this experience I felt compelled to tell my wife that if our marriage ended in divorce, I would be okay. It was my way of saying, 'If you feel you have to be here, please don't. You can leave, I understand.' She brushed it off and went about her day. I genuinely pushed forward with a new hope that we might be able to make our marriage work. After all we had a new baby that would arrive soon, whether anyone liked it or not. Our family was growing from five to six. I was really excited about our expected addition. I felt that my wife was unsure and hesitant about being back; it seemed as though she had reached her point of no return within our marriage. The unexpected pregnancy must have been a challenging twist in her life. I felt quite certain that, had the unexpected not happened, she would not have come back. For the time being we stuck it out. Actually the first couple of weeks were really enjoyable – until her parents decided it was time to meet with us for dinner. Their motivation was that my mother-in-law received a call to serve on a board for the women's society in the Mormon Church. It was a big deal for them, a big deal in their culture and lives. This new calling in the church apparently helped her grow a conscience. When we met them for dinner, my mother-in-law told us: 'After receiving my call to serve in the church I didn't want there to be any bad feelings.' Wow! Was this the first time they were verbalizing their bad feelings? And would we be sitting here right now if she hadn't been called to serve in the church? These were my thoughts – I certainly didn't say this out loud. The conversation soon turned towards me. They told me that I had offended them with what I had said over the years, and with who I had become. They also said it offended them when I drank alcohol around them. Last on their list of displeasures was: Was I trying to stop my wife from going to the Mormon temple? I responded that going to the temple was her decision; really it was no one else's business. Why they felt they needed to make it a part of their business was startling to me. It was like my wife and I were fifteen-year-olds being chastised for skipping out on our church duties. I had to remind myself that I was thirty-five years old. The arrogance of their beliefs asserted itself right in the face of our own marriage and our family. It was a display of how the church must come before any individual soul: if we can't control you and your actions, we still want to control your wife.

There was really nothing left for me to say. If I was going to make my marriage work, I had to somehow accept these people and all their insincere behavior. I didn't take it personally anymore, I accepted the fact that these were the cultural roles they had been playing their whole lives. It could have been anyone else in my shoes, it would have made no difference: anyone who challenged their cultural control would be seen as an obstacle on their daughter's path to salvation. To them, the future is much more important than the present, and those individuals who are not going where they are destined to go need to be removed or ignored. Somehow they dehumanize you. It is not personal; their beliefs are so egocentric that their actions are unconscious – they don't realize what they are doing.

A few days later I found out that my wife's brother was getting married in the temple in a few months. Now it made perfect sense why they had brought that up with me at dinner. My wife hadn't been to the temple in years: now that they were having a family gathering, they wanted all their children there. They were quietly letting me know that if my wife wasn't there on that day, I should know who they were going to blame. Rather than allowing each person to decide whether or not they would show up, they were exercising their control and manipulation. An individual's commitment to some higher power – or not – is their own business and nobody else's. This is something that should be highly personal, but they were once again putting it on public display. That never seemed like a very creative process to me.

I have read autobiographies and memoirs of individuals who have overcome difficulties, broken down barriers, set new records, challenged scientific boundaries, emancipated people from slavery, sought equality, climbed mountains never thought possible . . . Each of them had to find their own path; break from the old and into new territory. Whoever created us intended for us to be exactly that: creatures of creativity and beauty. If we evolve, the rest of humanity starts to evolve. How can it happen any other way?

I simply remained in my marriage. I was becoming more accepting within myself. My wife was pregnant and I was going to give it all I had; certainly our children deserved that. I continued the practice of observing my thoughts. I was surprised at how my mind slowed, the busy chatter of the past was fading. I often would laugh out loud in amusement at my ego and how it had worked in the past, a clingy neediness that wanted a label to be noticed. It was liberating to see it so clearly. And seeing myself clearly helped me see it in others, so my empathy and lack of judgment towards others slowly developed. Once I had tasted this sweet process, I could never go back. What would unfold in my life over the next year would eventually lead to the book you're holding in your hands.

No longer having regret over the past or anxiety over the future gave me the gift of being in the moment. With the shrinking global economy and the layoffs and cuts in health care, my business had dropped off by almost fifty percent in the span of two months. Added to that my inability to save for a rainy day and my insurmountable debt, and my small business was left drowning; I could no longer keep up. I desperately tried to secure a business consolidation loan to lower my initial outgoing expenses but it was a band-aid only, and I was quickly turned down. The only option left was to file personal bankruptcy, and this we did in August of 2008. Initially we thought we would be able to keep the house, but in the end that was too big of a burden, so the house was put into the bankruptcy as well. I felt grateful that I could still maintain my business and provide for my family. It could have been much worse. At the time we of course had no idea how long we would be able to stay in the house; all we could do was wait and see. My wife was very understanding and extremely supportive throughout the process. It wasn't her fault – I had made almost all our financial decisions, so it was all on my shoulders. I was very grateful for her support during this time. Before we actually lost some of our material possessions I had already let go of the desire to have them, so when it actually happened it was somewhat of a relief. The burden of being identified with things had been lifted. I was thankful for the whole process. The new awareness in my life created a bridge for me to cross. I was still unaware of the density of my pain from my childhood abuse. But bringing my shadows into the light was right around the corner.

Sundays had always been a very difficult day for me, as a child, as an adult, and in my marriage. Looking back on my childhood Sundays, these were days where spiritual abuse and physical abuse were mixed together. The two together caused a mixture of confusion, fear, and a tormenting of my young soul. The dark shadows were pieces of me that I had not yet fully discovered, afraid of what I might find. Beforehand I could not have handled the truth, that I was a broken thirty-something-year-old. Now it was time to look inward through the dark night, searching each shadow with the light of my own consciousness. My lack of judgment of myself allowed me to explore with courage and belief, rather than fear of what I previously did not want to see: the truth that I was abused and broken.

At this stage I had no knowledge of the kind of healing that I desperately needed. There were two Sundays within one month that I drank myself to total unconsciousness. It scared my wife and it scared the hell out of me. The day after the second bender I called a psychologist. I was sitting in his office within a week. It was the first visit of what would become many. It was finally a safe place for me, thank god, to completely open up. The trust for me was almost instantaneous. I was at a place in my life where I was completely open and ready to move forward. I knew I needed help.

It was November 2008. We now knew we would be having a little girl in January. We weren't at all surprised; in fact, before we knew the sex of the baby, my wife had a dream that it was a little girl and her name was Kate. I said, sounds great, if she is a girl, I agree, I love the name. That same month my wife told me it was her decision to go back to the Mormon temple. I knew she was doing it for her family; she was convinced that it was what she herself wanted. How could I possibly argue with that? I wanted her to travel her own path, whatever that may be; I simply felt it wasn't my place. I did make it very clear to her that I felt the church was coming before our marriage; she hastily disagreed. She moved forward with her decision, and it wasn't brought up again for several months.

In the first month of counseling I had four sessions that lasted an hour each. The timing was perfect and beautiful. The doors that were now opening I walked through with excitement and childlike anticipation. A year earlier I would have run for cover. It seemed as though the little boy who had been hiding his whole life was emerging. I could hear his voice whispering to me, Let go, it's okay to be who you are meant to be. The next few months I focused on the practice of non-judgment, and the new discovery of personal healing. It led me to a land of isolation, where I no longer felt that I related to many around me. Whereas beforehand I would have felt lonely, I now opened my arms to the feeling of aloneness. The fear of the truth that had covered me in a thick layer of mist and darkness disappeared as the light of truth poured in. The truth was setting me free; I was no longer afraid of it. I was no longer relating to old patterns of behavior. In the months that followed, I would simply listen to my inner spirit and no longer second-guess the call to be free.

The ending of old relationships and the welcoming of new ones had yet to happen – how that might unfold was something only time would sort out. In the event, it came much sooner than I could ever have guessed. Soon I would have to make choices that would leave me soaring and in freefall – the freefall at times lasting longer than I hoped for, but running and jumping right off the proverbial cliff was a decision I faced head-on. I felt as though I was taking action in my life, rather than reacting to life.

I had recently learned that a friend I hadn't spoken with for several years was going through a divorce. He was there for me six years earlier when my wife and I almost got a divorce; my affair, he knew all about it. He had shown up for me then, no judgment, he just listened and was a great friend. I felt that, if at all possible, I would like to return the same friendly support. There had been some distance between us, or, should I say, some bad blood. Neither one of us had ever let it go. I called him and left a message, asking if he would like to meet for lunch sometime. He called back the next day; we met for breakfast at the same place we had met six years earlier. Our histories were very similar: we both grew up in the Mormon Church, same community; both served Mormon missions; and we were both no longer attending church. It had been one month since he left his wife, and divorce proceedings were well underway. We had a great time catching up and discussing the similar path we had traveled, our feelings about the Mormon Church, our missions, our marriages – a lot was discussed in two short hours. I left our breakfast that morning admiring his courage to step away from his divided marriage – the same divided marriage I was in; the insanity of always feeling that you never measure up, that you are the one that fucked up your marriage because you decided that you no longer fit the mold of their religion; being the one everyone looks at differently, like there is a sign on your back that reads 'I haven't repented yet, until then keep treating me like I have leprosy.' The only time I could get my wife to see through this blind truth was as we left a gathering of non-Mormon friends. She said to me on the drive home, 'I feel like a fish out of water around those people.' I responded, 'Imagine feeling like that almost all of the time for the last seven years nonstop.' There was no response: she didn't agree or disagree.

My wife told me on a separate occasion that, when my older sister was in a church meeting with their bishop, my name somehow came up. The bishop responded 'Forget about him, he is too far gone.' I think even my wife was surprised by this. When this was passed on to me, I knew I no longer needed to give them and their opinions any energy. I knew how much fear they all lived with. I was very familiar with fear, and seeing this for the first time gave me a glimmer of empathy and understanding. It was no longer about me, none of it was personal: it was about them. It was their bundle of thoughts in their head. If they wanted to put that on me, fine, but I no longer had to buy in to their fear, guilt and control.

The wind was blowing, the leaves gently rustled, stirring my troubled soul. The opening of my hands allowed me to move with the wind and dance toward the unknown. I awoke early one morning with certainty that I needed to write, so I immediately put pen to paper, writing down the emotions I was feeling. I was writing with honesty; I held nothing back. My writing flowed like a river, with direction and meaning. I wrote about my surroundings – my family, my in-laws, my counseling, training – and through this process the clarity in my life blossomed like a beautiful flower. My journaling was in a way setting me free: I was finding solace and empowerment in pen and paper. One morning I awoke filled with inspiration and aliveness. I knew at that moment I had to leave Utah. Where to, I had no idea; when, I had no idea; how, no idea. Initially my feeling was that I needed to leave with my family if that was at all possible; my journal entry reads, 'I will leave with or without her, it's her path not mine.'

I was letting go without trying to let go. I didn't know at the time that I was letting go, yet it was happening all around me. I was thankful to my mentors and spiritual guides: their message was resonating like a ripple on a small pond. My counseling was opening up the shadows that I had spent my whole life running from. I began to confront the abuse and torment for the first time. In fact using the word 'abuse' was extremely difficult in the beginning – I constantly wanted to minimize what had happened to me. My other form of deflection in counseling was laughing about some of the terrifying incidents that had happened to me as a boy. I knew it was time to allow the truth to be accepted. I couldn't run any longer. My arrogant macho act was fading into the background. It was time to embrace the wounds that ran deep. I felt it was time to accept what I had found in my shadows. It was the only way to fully heal: to fulfill my divine creative call, I first must heal. I had moments of solitude and quiet where I wept, my body shaking uncontrollably. Those moments were beautiful. They opened up the process for new life to flourish within my weary soul.

I had decided to train for an ironman race: at the time it had seemed like the perfect outlet for my energies. I was now running thirty to fifty miles a week – I couldn't get enough. I was feeling free even in my running. My relationship with my wife was stagnant at best. The fighting and tension had virtually disappeared, which of course was refreshing considering the first eleven years of our marriage. The tension between me and my in-laws evaporated for me: I simply allowed it to be what it was. I no longer felt the need for their acceptance of me; and their quiet rejection was losing its grip. Accepting myself was more important than anyone else's acceptance.

Christmas came and went. The New Year arrived, and with it a blanket of fresh snow, the fluffy light kind that mirrored what I was feeling within. Our beautiful little Kate was born in January. She had almost a full head of dark hair like her mother's. I was once again filled with joy and excitement, holding Kate in my arms. It brought back memories of holding each one of my beautiful baby girls the day they arrived.

The moment of birth is an awakening itself: new life, new possibilities. Here is the very essence of creativity in a bundle of joy, hope with no past or regret, no judgment, just innocence. It is a reminder of the connectivity of all living things; and the beauty that flows through this intelligence is in everyone and everything. Nature flows this way, it winds and twists through everything we see and touch. The awe we witness every day can never be put in a box: how can we ever put life in a box when there are no right angles in nature?

Chapter 15

Divorce

It was a peaceful time in our marriage, everything on the surface seemed fine. Our lack of interest in each other was disconcerting, brought on perhaps by my training and my wife's decision to ramp up her religious commitments. I let go of my attachment to those in my life who no longer supported me. It was an effortless and natural process that at first I was unaware of. My retreat into myself allowed me to view relationships and circumstances in a whole new light. My ability to take action was gaining new strength. It wasn't through anything I did or said; it was what I didn't do. The observation of myself freed me from my unconscious thoughts and actions. Almost all of the relationships that needed to end would eventually end, virtually on their own. The drama that I had previously been so familiar with I could now step away from: I no longer made it into a problem.

In early February an opportunity arrived that initially proved to be very challenging. My oldest brother's small practice had also been downsizing, and he could no longer continue on his own. He asked me if I would allow him to practice in my office temporarily. Now our history of working together was shaky at best. I was younger and had a very difficult time telling him no, so this put me in a difficult position. My parents were still regularly pressuring me to stay within the guidelines of our family. My father had created this sense of entitlement towards my oldest brother – say yes to him and the family support would be there – but I, on the other hand, would be miserable with the new arrangements. Say no, and the divisions in the family would begin, led by my father – and I knew on which side of the division I would fall. I clumsily told my brother no. It was clumsy because it was the first time in my life that I had told him no. After a couple of texts telling me that I had turned my back on family, the relationship tacitly ended once again.

I was learning that when we place expectations on relationships and circumstances, the flow of that relationship or situation falls out of alignment with the cycle of life. The relationship is cut off from its true source; growth and expansion are not possible. I felt at peace with my decision: I felt as though I had narrowly escaped selling myself short. It was a close call. What followed was what I had expected. The gathering support my oldest brother received from my parents was a clear indication that the drama of family dysfunction was something that needed this kind of energy to keep it going. I no longer wanted any part in that cycle of insanity. At family gatherings, generally whoever wasn't present was made fun of, talked about, laughed at. I had fully participated in this family behavior many times in the past; I was perhaps one of the worst offenders. Now it no longer served a purpose for me, that path for me ended. I had a moment of clarity that told me, not only are you breaking free from your religion, you are also breaking free of the relationships that no longer empower you, that no longer serve your higher self.

During this opening in my life I could also start to heal from the abuse. The wounds were deep but somehow I knew that I could bring them to the light of my own awareness, my acceptance of the truth. Allowing my wounds to surface would be a journey that at times I would seriously call into question. Realizing the strength I had would only come through experiences that at times damn near killed me. Surviving the experience was the lesson that would transform the prior limitations I had set on myself. Those limitations were conditioned cultural responses to thought, rather than action towards the gentle flow of life.

My relationship with my wife continued to be at a standstill; we were essentially coexisting. She was not going where I was going and I could never go back to what she was still so much a part of. We were now heading in increasingly separate directions. We talked about moving out of the state, and initially she was on board – she wasn't exactly doing cartwheels, but she was open to the idea. As our commitment to each other continued to slide, her resistance to moving away from her family or out of the state grew stronger. I was somewhat surprised but not really. I told her it was okay, she didn't have to move. It was during this conversation that I realized our marriage was over. I didn't say anything to her at the time – truthfully, the knowledge hadn't fully sunk in – but it was like the last tumble fell into place. How it would play out, I had no idea. If the path was a divorce then I would walk that lonely path.

The friend I had reconnected with was now living with his girlfriend out in New York State. We had spoken on the phone a few times, and this had given me some idea of how difficult a divorce can be – the pain, the separation, guilt about not being there for the children. My first thought was the kids, of course, especially Kate, being so small. But I couldn't allow myself to think about what would be or could be: the future would sort itself out. I hadn't heard from my oldest brother in almost two months – the perceived friendship of our relationship was blown open.

I didn't know it at the time, but the last weekend in March 2009 would be the last weekend I would spend living with my wife and kids. It was the weekend that baby Kate was to receive her blessing in the church. My father-in-law was giving her the blessing. I showed up to be there, and as soon as it was over I quickly left. The blessing is right before they open the floor to everyone who would like to bear testimony. My father almost always gets up, and I knew that I couldn't be there for this. It was a trigger that opened up deep wounds from my youth. After the baby blessing and church service, my in-laws and family met at our house. These gatherings were usually very uncomfortable; thankfully this would be the last gathering of this kind that I would attend.

Going back was no longer an option. The way forward needed only one fact: tell the truth. I spent the following Tuesday afternoon listing my emotional, spiritual and physical ideals for a mate. The list I made startled me. I saw my counselor right after compiling my list and I let him know all about it. I was scared, yet filled with a sense of relief. I went home that evening and asked my wife if she would like to make her own list, and she agreed. The next day I reconnected with my oldest brother after two months of not hearing from him. I told him I might be getting a divorce. I think he was surprised, mainly at the fact that I was okay with the decision. It felt good to finally take some type of action, action that to many might have seemed reckless and irresponsible. I was no longer concerned with the opinions others might have of me. This was my life and it was time to take responsibility for my own choices, even if that led to a divorce. I could no longer live with the rejection from family, my in-laws, and the community: I had reached the end of that path. I was ready to let go without any resentment or blame. I saw our marriage now from a different perspective. There was no blame to go around, it was simply the culture and the rigid beliefs that create such a difficult environment for a marriage like ours to exist without division.

I began this spiritual journey believing that if I could become a better person then everything would be better. If I had known beforehand that certain relationships would end, I might not have continued. When we start to see our life as it really is, it is very easy to retreat. The changes and what we must confront can be daunting. When true transformation has taken place, though, how can old relationships remain the same? Other people in your life understand the changes and accept the fact that you are no longer wanting the same things you used to want. If acceptance is not present, your paths diverge in separate directions. Your family know your old self so well that they have the hardest time letting go of the old you. The old version of you is what they have always identified with, and it flies in the face of what they are comfortable with. But it is only their fear that wants to hold on to the old. They may say they want the best for you; what they are really saying is, I want what is best for me. True change frightens most people – within themselves, and also in others. It represents leaving the comfort of the known. It's okay for this to be this way, it's nice when we become aware of this. Then true empathy and love for each other can naturally emerge in all good relationships.

Thursday morning my wife and I sat down and talked. She had made her list, and had come to a similar conclusion: I was not completely what she wanted in a partner. I asked her if she was ready to go forward with a divorce; she said that she was. I wasn't surprised. I did think she would want me around a little longer because of the baby, but it wasn't to be. We agreed that I would move out on Saturday; we would tell the children Saturday morning.

I was happy that we agreed mutually to end our marriage – although the mutual part would slowly start to unravel over the next few weeks. My wife's position was right smack in the middle: the decision to have a divorce was not her own: ownership of any choice wasn't a part of her vocabulary. Making an individual decision inside this culture is not possible; your decisions are made for you. I had left the Mormon Church and wasn't coming back. She also knew that she would have the full support of both families and of the community. I on the other hand would receive the full weight of rejection. That evening I called and told my parents that we were getting a divorce. The matter-of-fact way I told my father left little room for him to offer his opinion. It took them by surprise, although our difficult marriage over the years hadn't been a secret. My wife also told her family, and they weren't surprised. I guessed their joy in the demise of our marriage brought some relief: the person that offended them would no longer be in their lives. I would never hear from anyone in her family again. This I fully expected from them – I was all too aware of their conditional love. But to discover that my own family considered me dispensable would come as a shock.

My friend in New York, knowing the difficulty that lay ahead for me in Utah, extended the invitation to fly out and stay with him and his girlfriend. I booked a trip for the next week – a little space would go a long way.

Before my wife and I parted, she asked me only once if I was having an affair of any kind. I told her that I couldn't leave my marriage, or my children for that matter, with the influence of someone else in my life. I had learned my lesson more than six years ago. I had to do this on my own for it to be right – if there is such a thing as right. I wouldn't allow anyone or anything to interfere with the unfolding of this new journey. I needed a clear conscience to shoulder the attacks that I knew were coming. I just didn't know those attacks would come so close to home. I loved my wife and I always will – she is an incredible woman, beautiful in so many ways. We just found ourselves caught in the insanity of a rigid controlling culture that has lost the very essence of what love is. Instead of loving the individual for who they are and what they can become, allowing beauty to grow, they are like an angry gardener, frustrated that the tree is growing too fast or not in the direction the gardener wants it to grow. Gardeners create beautiful gardens; however the awe and splendor in nature a gardener can never create.

Race morning arrived. I was filled with the pre-race jitters, but also a strong sense of calm about the decision to end our marriage. It was a cold morning the first week in April and gently snowing. I felt perhaps the thin fresh blanket of snow somehow represented new life, embracing new places, new people, a new perspective, perfect, I thought. Everything had changed – or was it that everything remained the same, and what had changed was me? I was delighted at the end of the race to see my kids – my wife had brought them along. It was a reminder of her kindness and good heart. Perhaps if we had lived in a different state or country our marriage would have had a different ending. It wasn't to be: this was our path and the time we spent together was exactly that, the time we needed to, nothing more, nothing less. The creation of four beautiful daughters was perhaps the only reason we came together. I suspect it wasn't the only reason, but I can't think of one that's better.

Chapter 16

Closure and Exploration

After some coffee and hot chocolate and high fives all around, I reluctantly got into my car and drove towards the house. I would be leaving that afternoon. Was I ready was the only question I could think of. Was I ready to confront my children, the innocent bystanders in the ending of their parents' marriage? I imagined it doesn't get any tougher than this, this is a tall order. I was about to shatter their innocent little world.

I walked into the living room. I saw my children busily enjoying a regular Saturday morning that was about to become anything but regular. I paused for a moment and breathed in: this was the last time I would observe my children in this way. It was a sobering moment, perhaps the most difficult moment in my life. But on the other hand I had a strong resolve: I must continue with our decision. Strangely I felt that, between my wife and me, there was now mutual respect for each other as our marriage ended. Maybe this came through our acceptance that we were now in two totally different worlds – there was nothing left to fight about or say. I had prepared a letter the day before, to give my wife when I left. I didn't want to leave with any anger or resentment; I wanted there to be only love and acceptance. I knew this would be healthy for the both of us and of course for our children.

I called the girls down to join my wife and myself. Everything for me slowed down. I saw the look on my oldest daughter's face – it was a look that seemed to know exactly what was coming, like she had always known and feared its arrival. Her shift in energy seemed to transform her younger sisters too. I watched in agony as their playful Saturday mood changed. I felt helpless, yet keenly aware of their every move. It immobilized me for just a second, and my wife appeared shaky too. I would be the one to verbalize the severing of their parents. The aftermath we watched in silence, unable to comfort our children. The tears streamed down their cheeks; my wife was crying too. I sat in silent awareness of the emotional shock my daughters were displaying. It lasted maybe fifteen minutes, but it felt like hours. Watching the scene before me tore at every heart string that was not yet broken, the angst in wanting it to be different for them stamped a determination in my soul to write the truth. I vowed in that moment to walk away with a silent truce to soar for them. A picture of words that would unveil an image of freedom and beauty. Not a bird soaring high above the clouds – better yet, an example of human indifference triumphantly being exposed for the world to see. A message of healing resonating a promise that the truth within you sets you free.

We had previously decided that we would not hire attorneys. I would take my personal belongings and leave her the rest. I was ready to let go of everything; none of the material things served my needs anymore, I no longer wanted to carry that heavy burden. My new life was at one with life, so I felt the call to let it all go.

Loading my few belongings into my car took only so long, while the children attended to their Saturday activities. It occurred to me that in my childhood I had the ungodly hope that my father and mother would split up – this is rare in most child–parent relations. I know it was with my children. The next day confirmed this to me. I was on a Sunday hike with a friend I was staying with, when my cell phone rang: it was six-year-old Sophie. We talked for a few minutes, then she began to cry. She asked me who would tuck her in at night. I mustered up the courage to tell her, 'Mommy will.' We hung up and I lost it. I sat down on an outcrop of rocks overlooking the city and cried like a small boy. It was a moment I will never forget, a moment when my decision to get a divorce was tested to the core. The new reality was pouring in. Thank god I had made the choice to be honest with my marriage. The old me who lied to himself would have folded like a deck of cards. Knowing the way was no longer my motto: one shaky foot in front of the other would be a better description.

The first few days of being gone were very difficult. Being alone for the first time in twelve years without my children around was overwhelming. A good friend of mine had offered her home for me to stay in until I got my feet on the ground. She had lost her husband from an unexpected heart attack. I had been somewhat of a support for her, and our friendship had developed through grief and healing. In addition she was a Mormon who no longer wanted to be one. It was initially a good place for me to land: her place was in a different community than mine, and I felt that the space I would need over the coming weeks to months would be critical. My friend was a huge support, one I leaned on heavily. I never questioned whether my decision to leave was right or wrong: it was something I knew I had to do. What amazed me more than anything was that it brought calmness and peace.

I was headed for New York. I needed to go somewhere I had never been before, a place to clear my head, no pressure, a spot to just be. I was scared and excited at the same time. I had a long day of travel ahead of me – time to think and to be alone was something I was looking forward to. Flying alone was one step towards overcoming many small hurdles that my safe little world had protected me from. Each step would be a prelude to bigger hurdles that were sure to come. Surviving each one would hold the key to living a life without limitations.

When I landed in New York City, I was overwhelmed with a sense of new adventure. My good friend and his girlfriend were waiting for me. He was holding a map of downtown New York: with a Sharpie he had written in large lettering 'MORMON RE-HAB'. We laughed pretty hard. It was our little joke, although it ran very deep. Being able to laugh at it was the best part. We drove at least an hour north of the city. I just sat back and enjoyed the ride. I had expected city after city, but now we were out in the country. I awoke the next morning and walked out on the deck in the backyard to the most beautiful green expanse of trees I had ever seen. There were even a couple of deer grazing in the yard. I was blown away. In Utah you can see for miles; here I couldn't see more than a few hundred yards in any direction I looked. That day we spent some time in New Jersey. Everything was a fresh new experience for me, and I received it all with open arms. We spent the evening with some of their friends at a local bar and grill, and everyone I met was extremely welcoming and very nice. I was on a high from all the new experiences.

The next morning I wanted to go on a run, so my friends drew a map of a route in the country. The entire loop was just shy of seven miles. Off I went with my small map and a cell phone in case I got lost. I began my run excited yet hoping I didn't lose my way in an area that I was so unfamiliar with. To my surprise I was running in the most beautiful country I had ever seen. The trees were so thick, the forest floor was its own greenery and garden. I saw deer, woodchuck, squirrels, turtles – it was amazing. It felt more remote than my small community back in Utah. I literally cried, laughed, and felt the mother of creation embrace my soul. It was as though each birdsong, the smell of nature, was meant for me. I felt connected and grounded to the earth. When I thought of my children and their mother back in Utah, my eyes filled up with tears. Then as the tears dried up, I felt an intense joy at the aliveness of the moment as it cradled me in its loving embrace. It was an experience I had tasted before, but this time it was staying with me, increasing in intensity in proportion to what I was letting go of. When I got back, I burst through the door. My friend asked me 'How was it?' and I told him what I have just written, almost word for word.

I was riding the highs and I would quickly learn to ride the lows, too. My healing had only just begun. To fully heal from my childhood would of course take some time. I would need to get a perspective that would rise above the fray, so I could see the way things really happened. Seeing the impersonal nature of everything allows the spirit of forgiveness to flow into our lives. This was part of the path: I was here to forgive and to love.

That evening the three of us ventured into the city, where I became overwhelmed and depleted. The shock of my rapidly changing life, combined with my unfamiliar surroundings, closed in around me. It felt like a deep, dark abyss had opened wide and I was being pulled into it. A sense of panic and uncertainty overwhelmed me, closing in on me fast. The thought of death, and not making it, held me prisoner to thoughts in the past that I had not let go of yet. Thank god I was in the safe haven of friends. My friend bought some cookies and a can of Coke. I was unaware that I hadn't eaten at all that day: in the shock of my new life I had forgotten the most basic of life's needs. I consumed what I could, not tasting much of anything. The pull towards that dark hole loosened its grip on me. The mixture of emotion, my unfamiliar surroundings, and the fact that I had depleted my energy stores had caused a panic attack. Whatever it was, with the help of loving friends I managed to regain myself.

I was surviving each small step. This was crucial for me to learn. I had been that scared, unsure little boy my entire life, and I needed the experience of the unknown to blow the doors off my own limitations. The small steps had to come before the big steps. Retreating to my old self and comforts was no longer an option. I trusted the process, I trusted the universe. I could finally start to hear its call. The doors that needed to open would open: all I had to do was walk through them. No stress or strain; in fact the beauty of the process was that it was becoming just the opposite – effortless. My conditioned past was the only thing that could slow me down, and that was losing its grip. The melting away of my old life would be accelerated by my family – sooner than I ever could have imagined. Their world and my new world were inevitably going to collide, it was only a matter of when.

My trip out to the East Coast was winding down. I had enjoyed my time with friends who could relate to a whole new world of events, and I was grateful to them for listening and understanding me. We hugged, and I flew back to Utah that Sunday afternoon. I knew that the next three months would be critical for me. I wanted to be with my girls as much as I could, and I needed to finalize the divorce. My goal was to get out of Utah as soon as I could. Of course at the time I wasn't certain about any steps I would need to take. I was open to any and all possibilities. I figured it would take at least a year before I could pick up and move. My timeline was certainly not aligned with that of the universe.

I returned to my new living arrangements with a little hope that everything would work out. Before I left to the East Coast I had received one phone call from my father. He was calm yet very manipulative in his tone. I just listened. He told me that I was losing control of my life and situation; that my wife would be successful and her family wouldn't let her fail. I responded, 'I'm happy for her, I actually want to see her become successful.' As I hung up the phone I realized I no longer needed control; it was okay to let go of it. I was happy that all aspects of control in my life were coming to an end – not just letting go of my own control issues, but letting go of relationships where others tried to control me. I no longer had a part to play in the emotional drama. After severing my marriage, I felt that any other relationship that held me captive would simply end. The demise of dysfunction would allow me to spread my wings further. I had jumped off the cliff; now I desperately needed new wings to fly.

Midweek I called my wife to ask her when we could start the divorce papers and meet with a mediator. The conversation quickly turned to how she suspected I was having an affair with my roommate, who was fifty-four. I was speechless. I really didn't see this coming – especially when I learned that my own parents were stoking the fire. They had asked all of my brothers if they had any information about me having an affair. I felt as though I was sitting in a chair. The storm clouds rolled in, darkness, the lightning and thunder were all around me. It was pouring sheets of rain. I sat and watched the storm; I was unmoved, untouched. I was in the eye of the storm and I was perfectly fine. This gave me courage and strength. It came from a place of stillness that I already knew was there. I no longer invested any energy in accusations or drama of any kind.

My roommate felt it would be best for both of us if I found somewhere else to live. The door opened wide: a friend of ours made one call, and that same day I found a great spot to move my few belongings to. I was renting a basement apartment from another widow. She was a kind, gracious lady who welcomed me with open arms. Her encouragement for me to follow the path was exactly what I needed. My intention was to stay for six months and then reevaluate my situation.

It was now mid April. I was running consistently and still training for some triathlons that were quickly approaching. The training was a great release for all that was going on, all the changes in my life. During my long runs I could hear inspiring thoughts that flowed to me like I was speaking on a stage, words that I had never read or written. I spoke them to myself and then out loud – it would sometimes last for five miles. I barely even knew that I was running: my feet seemed to float above the ground. I wrote these thoughts down in my journal – it seemed to be the only place I could express all that I needed to at that moment. The flow of words was so consistent that I ached with anticipation for its birth. I was seeing flashes of my life all the way from my childhood to the present. It was a timeline that made perfect sense. The time to write the book I could not find had arrived.

It took one small trip in my car to move my belongings to my new place. I still had some personal things at my wife's home – things like high-school yearbooks, family pictures, all my Mormon mission memories in one box, also my stamp collection that I had carted around since I was a little boy, a couple of snowboards – the kind of stuff you never throw away, but never really pull out and look at. I would gather these things later. For now I needed to keep it simple, so I could pack up and move when the time was right. My new landlady was kind enough to allow me to pay my rent month to month. This was perfect: I didn't want to sign a lease of any kind. The lease where my office was located had finished the previous year, so I was also month to month there. I really was footloose and fancy-free. It felt right, it was exactly the way it needed to be. My new apartment was surrounded by trees, which is rare in Utah. I felt that my new spot was safe and full of healing energy. I knew that I would need the safety and healing over the ensuing months. I was close to the college where I swam in the pool a few times a week, and the weather was warming, so I could get back to running outside. The distance from my old life to this one was far enough for now. I hadn't heard from my parents in two weeks; had only spoken to maybe three of my nine siblings. My wife's tone was now changing. I learned from her that my father had encouraged her to get an attorney. I was a little bewildered – his style of play hadn't changed in all these years. My parents contacted me – or should I say my mother did. It was superficial contact at best. The little bits and pieces I was hearing about my father were surfacing. So you could say I was very wary of trusting my parents. Being well aware of my father's manipulative influence on most of my siblings, I was careful who I spoke with.

Chapter 17

Flowing like a Gentle River

I spent an entire morning meditating on the beauty of a flower and the likeness that existed in the flower and myself. I studied the way the flower sways back and forth under a gentle breeze – there is no resistance – and I thought how I could learn to be like this too. My oldest brother showed up minutes after my reflection. I was in a good spot, very grounded at that moment. My brother, perhaps out of concern for me, asked me in a panicked tone if I had considered what might happen in my divorce. I could lose everything, he told me, my wife might take me to the cleaners, I would be left with nothing. I listened to everything he said to me. When he was finished, I simply said, 'Whatever happens I'm okay with the outcome, because it won't change who I am.' It changed the tone in the room, he actually agreed. The topic never came up again.

Once again my brother arrived at my apartment. At this time he was the one I spoke to the most in my family, he made himself readily available, so the information about my parents was coming from him. Support from the rest of my family had been virtually nonexistent. My father was scurrying around the family, including my wife, seeing which siblings would turn their back on me. I hadn't spoken with my older sister, who was only fourteen months older than me, since leaving my wife. She had seen and heard enough from our father. She called him out on his behavior – how could he treat his son this way, calling him names, things I had no knowledge of. She was witnessing the insanity and was saying enough is enough. My brother was filling me in on his version of this developing story. All of a sudden I found myself defending my sister, mainly because my brother didn't like her approach. Immediately I became aware that my oldest brother was not there for me. I decided just to observe his brotherly support – if there was any.

I felt I needed to give my sister a call; she beat me to it. After having a really great conversation with her, I knew that she was full of genuine love. We were speaking the same language. I was amazed at who emerged to show love and compassion: my sister was one of them, and I welcomed her support. The fact that she stood up to the bullying tactics of our father put her in his crosshairs: losing control of one of his pawns was not something he was used to.

I was feeling sorry for my father. I felt some empathy for him in the hell he was creating for himself. To divide and control takes huge amounts of energy. It was almost a full-time job for him. I visualized my father playing a game of chess by himself; all ten of his children were his pawns. I fully believed he wanted what he saw as the best for each pawn; the world of fear and control gave him only a limited perspective. The suffering he created for himself and those who chose to participate would continue. Stepping outside of this insane cycle gave me space to observe what I had for a long time viewed as normal behavior. It would never be personal for me anymore, though. How could it be?

Three and a half years ago my father had a heart attack. He was one of the lucky ones – he didn't die. It led to a triple bypass, open-heart surgery. It was a shock to our family, a scare as to how fragile life can be. All of my siblings and their spouses were gathered around my father in the ICU. A machine was methodically breathing for him, his large chest was moving slowly up and down. I remember thinking how helpless my father looked – without modern technology he would be dead. It was a sobering moment. All of my siblings were crying, as was my wife. I, though, felt almost no emotion. Why wasn't I crying? What was wrong with me? Minutes after the ICU experience, I was heading back to my office when it hit me: I cried really hard. I was alone now and the tears flowed. I always felt that my father's emotional baggage would lead to a heart attack. I thought it that day in Australia when he was pressing me up against the window. The truth was at this moment I wasn't ready to lose my father. Perhaps the fact that I hadn't forgiven him and healed was at the core of my emotions. It presented a real challenge for me to heal from the abuse and move forward. I was more determined than ever: I made a promise to myself, that day, I would find a way to forgive and heal, no matter how long it took.

After the surgery it was of course a slow recovery. There was a new gentleness in my father that had never been there before. It was fairly easy to be around him. The ego had temporarily been put to rest. It lasted perhaps six months. As my father slowly regained his strength there was an emergence of the old judgment and control – it was like it had never really left. The thickening of the old ego seemed even more coarse and less tolerant than before. I felt within myself that he had lost an opportunity to strip away some of those layers, to emerge softer, gentler than before, perhaps even to begin to heal from his childhood wounds. The black-and-white paradigm of his religious beliefs traps you inside a room, inside a box, where the freedom to explore your shadows is left no room. The shadows are ignored and never explored; they must be forgotten. This traps the energy of healing, so the burden continues to run your life; escaping its pain becomes almost impossible.

The family dynamics were fairly uneventful over the next few weeks. I stayed busy with my practice and my training. My wife and I were now exchanging the girls every other weekend – we fell into a comfortable routine. I was enjoying every moment I had alone with my girls. I would see little Kate only briefly when I picked up the other kids and dropped them off. I held her as long as I could, and I cried every time I drove away. It was difficult leaving them. It was something that I had chosen to do, temporarily, and I would learn to get used to it. It gave me some alone time to contemplate each one of my girls, what I loved and appreciated in their individual personalities. We had a lot of fun when we were together. I took them to an amusement park, won them all a little stuffed toy tiger. It was a little bit of normal that we all desperately needed. We went to the park, fed the ducks. We always had movie night on Saturday nights – I let them watch whatever movie they wanted to. The best part was the king-size bed I had in my apartment. All four of us would squeeze into the bed and go to sleep. Every moment I had with them was precious we didn't waste a minute of our time together.

My time alone was spent reading, running, or writing in my journal. I felt the desire to put my practice up for sale – it was only a thought; I wasn't quite ready for it. I checked out the possibility of getting my license in New Jersey – other than a few hoops to jump through it seemed easy enough. In what capacity I would practice out on the East Coast I had no idea, but I remained open to the idea. My counseling continued. I needed it – the process for me to fully heal had just begun. I wasn't going to let go of that yet, not until I was ready. I would know when that was.

My older brothers and I had a triathlon that was fast approaching, and I took my daughters to the race. It was a five-hour drive south, in southern Utah. It was now early May, and the race was on a Saturday. We drove down Thursday. It was great being with my girls; towards the end of the drive the noise level was gradually escalating until I was almost ready to return them to their mother – and the trip had only just begun. After a few empty threats the noise went down a notch or two. When we arrived at the hotel, all my girls wanted to do was swim and play with their cousins. It was great to see them having so much fun.

The race was my first open-water swim ever. When we arrived at the lake the wind was blowing; the water was anything but flat. With my buoyant wetsuit and all, I got a little way out into the water, maybe a hundred yards. I panicked, then headed immediately back to the shoreline. I had had enough for one day. The next day we swam again: this time I froze; I wouldn't swim across this choppy little channel of water. After at least ten minutes of coaxing from my two older brothers I swam with anxiety. They both stayed close to me, they were great at helping me that day. I felt like I had overcome a big fear.

The next morning was the race. I was deathly scared of the swim portion, which was a mile in length. I was far from confident, especially with a few hundred other bodies in the water. We arrived the morning of the race: the wind was howling, there were whitecaps on the lake, everyone stood around in their wetsuits. The race organizers waited almost two hours before calling off the swim. So my first and only triathlon quickly became a duathlon. Run bike run – I wasn't one of the competitors complaining, actually I was smiling. I ended up finishing the race. I was happy with the experience and, more importantly, my girls were there to see their dad cross the finish line.

The next Saturday I was once again running in the local half marathon. The gun was going off only a couple of miles from my parents' house and they let me stay the night. There was an undercurrent of contempt towards me, mainly from my father. My parents had been at the last race, so I had seen them a couple of times, but I never brought up what my father had been saying to the rest of the family about me – I felt that it would be a waste of time and energy. As long as they treated me personally with some decency and respect, then they would see me. Being once again at my parents' the night before the same race as a year earlier brought back a flood of memories from when my wife had left with the kids and moved in with her family. The circle of events was fascinating to observe.

I was in much better shape this year than the previous year, and I was anxious to see how much I would improve my time. My older sister was running in the race as well, and it was great seeing her proudly compete with a smile – a little moral support. I felt prepared and ready to go. The race was underway. I felt really good. It was perfect weather, a little brisk but great for a half marathon. At about the nine-mile mark in the race I felt the trees all around me breathing beautiful oxygen into my lungs. I welcomed with gratitude the exchange between two living beings. As I was in this state of gratitude the wind picked up, the trees rustled with excitement. The breeze blew me all the way to the finish line. I shed tears as I finished the race. It was like the universe was cradling me in recognition that I was on the right path. I set a personal record that day: I had beat my time the year before by twenty-one minutes. The best part was getting a picture with my girls at the finish line – my wife had brought them to my race. It was awkward for her, but she had managed to set her own feelings aside for our daughters.

I went home to my lonely little apartment. I was getting used to being on my own. I was reading a lot of books and studying my favorites. I would need to draw on my own strength and what I had learned over the last year, more than ever before. The storm clouds would once again circle in my life. Would I have enough fortitude and presence to weather the storm that I somehow knew was coming?

The following Wednesday my wife and I felt that we had come to a reasonable agreement. We met with our attorney and our petition for divorce was filed. She would get full custody of our children, with joint legal custody. I still kept all of my visitation rights. We agreed on alimony and child support. I was at a point where I just wanted the divorce so we could both move forward with our lives. That same week I booked a trip to New York to visit my friends again. I specifically chose the Fourth of July weekend, as it's my favorite holiday and I knew that my kids would be busy with their mom and her family that day. I was still speaking with my sister on a regular basis. I hadn't heard from anyone else in my family other than my two older brothers whom I was still training with.

I was doing another triathlon that Saturday, and we wanted to scope out the course. We arrived at the small manmade lake where the swim was to be held. I was keen to try and overcome my fear of the open water. We headed into the murky water. My brothers were full of excitement and anticipation; I on the other hand was filled with dread. They took off. I felt okay, I was just a little behind them. When we had gone a couple of hundred yards they veered left towards the middle of the lake. I decided to head back – I didn't want to have a panic attack in the water, though as it turned out I had no choice in the matter. I made a direct line for some rocks along the shore, midway to my original destination. Dragging myself up on the rocks, I was able to gather myself and slow my breathing. When I looked around I realized that to get back to my original spot I would have to swim, there was no other option. It was maybe seventy-five yards. I slipped back into the water, mustering up whatever courage I had left. I must have only gone twenty to thirty yards out when the panic set back in. I thought I was going to die – my heart was thumping almost out of my chest. I knew I could make it, but god, I needed to calm down. If it wasn't for the buoyancy in my wetsuit, I'm quite sure I would have drowned. I put my head down and just kept swimming. When I reached the old broken-down boat ramp I slid my shaky body up the slimy cement remains and lay there in shock. I knew in that moment I couldn't continue doing this to myself. I was drowning in emotional grief; feeling like I was physically drowning was simply too much for me at the time. I was done, I knew I had to be. There were other things I had to focus on; this was too far down the list of priorities. Doing triathlons was my brothers' thing and I had tried hard to make it mine, but really all I wanted to do was run. Giving it up was an easy decision, and one I never regretted.

Moving from the shadows had to happen in all aspects of my life. Being in my older brothers' shadows was one aspect that was long overdue for retirement. It certainly wasn't their fault; it was my desperate attempt to get recognition from my father, but recognition and approval from him was something I would never get. Accepting this gave me comfort and a feeling of liberation. I was overjoyed to no longer be seeking validation from those who could never validate me. Before we can accept anyone for who they are, we must first have total acceptance of ourselves.

That weekend I spent some time with good friends who fully accepted me for who I was, and I was introduced to some other people who quickly became amazing support for me. Certain people seem to show up in our lives for specific reasons. Some of those people remain; others are there just for a brief moment, then they are gone. The ability to accept this, then let go when it's time to let go, allows us to blossom on our path.

I was supposed to pick up my girls on Sunday, the day before Memorial Day, but my wife and I had a miscommunication on time and I didn't arrive. My kids were upset, my wife was upset. I apologized and we arranged that I would pick them up on Memorial Day morning. I was happy to have my girls for the holiday. I took them to the movies, we grabbed some lunch – it was a memorable day for all of us. My mother called and asked if we wanted to come over for a barbeque, a last-minute thing my parents had put together. We picked up a few items at the grocery store and headed to my parents' house a little early. We were the first to arrive – and we were the first to leave. When we got there I immediately picked up on my father's negative energy. Apparently I wasn't the only one who noticed; later my brother said that our mother called him and told him to hurry up and get to the house because 'your father's on one'. The mood deteriorated rapidly. My father was making fun of the new life I had chosen. I could see that he was losing control. My children were in the room, so naturally my eyes were scanning the room for a quick exit. He left the room for a few minutes, perhaps to cool down. While he was out, I told my mother that I was officially done. I felt that I had no choice: I could no longer accept any form of abuse. At this point my father returned and attacked me with renewed vigor – he was no longer in control of himself. He told me that I was a narcissistic failure, that I had failed at everything in my life. I immediately gathered our belongings and headed for the door. It was a replay of my teenage years: I was flashed back to the torrent of verbal abuse that I had been so familiar with; the difference now was that my daughters were in the room. I left, with a feeling of resolve that I would have to sever this kind of relationship if I was to follow the path I was on. My love for my parents would remain. The difference was that looking for any validation from either was finally over.

My girls asked me what had just happened. I told them, this is the result of not accepting people for who they are. I told them, no matter who they become I would always embrace them and love them – no strings attached of any kind. We had a couple of hours left before I needed to drop them off at their mother's. We went and got ice creams and sat by a beautiful river. We got a great picture of us there. We were happy to be together and in a good spot.

The river spoke to my inner soul: Travel your course, follow your path. There will always be resistance, expect it. The pristine flowing river reflected an image of water being brought to the dry lips of a weary traveler. Together we will embrace the essence of quenching thirst. The watery stillness comes from a large body of water, a reservoir of potential relief – water being the element of healing along with sustaining life. The river is always moving towards another source of water giving life along its winding journey. We are life and when we give our love we become like a river bringing solace to many weary travelers.

Chapter 18

Unfolding Life's Purpose

I dropped my daughters off that night. My wife was a little confused as to why I had brought them home early. I told her, 'I'm sure you'll hear all about it.' The version she would get from the rest of my family didn't surprise me; the only part that was unsettling was that my oldest daughter was denying what had happened at my parents'. It would develop on its own, I would give it no energy. My oldest daughter said to me later that I was a liar, that Grandpa would never lie. I left it at that – I knew what I was dealing with. There was nothing to resist or fight anymore; I simply let it be. I would remain silent on the whole matter.

The severing of my relationship with my parents seemed to accelerate the path I was on. If leaving my nest was to be a part of my journey, then I would leave. The next day I officially put my practice up for sale. I priced it below what I had originally intended – I wasn't expecting to get much for it. Within three days of advertising the sale of my business, I received a call from a serious buyer in the form of a voicemail. My heart skipped a beat. I thought to myself, am I ready to let go of my last safety net? It took me two days to return his call, and he was on his way to visit my practice the next week.

When I told my oldest brother I had a potential buyer for my office, the squeeze was on. He asked me to consider selling my practice to him. He offered what he could – a percentage of the collections in the first year – but I told him that I had to put my wife and kids first. I needed a lump sum of money to pay my alimony and child support, until I got my feet on the ground. I felt that my decision to put my children first was an easy one. But my brother then said to me, 'You always think of yourself, no one else,' and he hung up on me. His motivation was now revealed, front and center. I was going through what was perhaps the toughest period of my life – almost my entire family had deserted me in one week – and now they showed up to see what was in it for them. It was staggering to watch. I watched it all unfold from the sidelines. My sister remained close, watching it with me. I wasn't upset, I was just perplexed that I had been part of this dysfunctional family for so long. I was leveled by an email I received from my brother that summed up the nature of our long-time dysfunctional relationship. It simply deserved no response. I no longer needed to suffer in this way.

The distance I now had from my family would open doors I had never dreamed possible. As painful as it was at times, as old relationships dissolved a whole new expanse unfolded like a beautiful flower. My arms were wide open, my hands flat, a gentle wind was blowing. I could hear the rustling of the leaves. I was going in the direction of the wind. Not knowing my destination was the best part – I no longer needed to know. The expanse of the horizon offered a safer view than the world I was leaving behind. I was starting a new chapter in my life, and this time I would make sure that I would be the author. If I stumbled, then so be it: I could now say that I was the one who stumbled. If I failed, my failure would be my lesson and my lesson alone.

The support I needed arrived at just the right moment. It came in the form of a handful of individuals who believed in me and my call to be free. I was open to all ways of healing, and I felt that the time had arrived to draw on the energy of guides and healers. A friend of mine was a shaman healer, and one Friday morning I arrived at her house. We talked for a while about some of the events that had unfolded in my life. She had an in-depth understanding of the Mormon culture and this gave her insight into my life. She was completely without judgment. She taught me to send love from my higher self to everyone, including my family. I felt lightness all over my body. I was soaring, somehow gliding through my own consciousness. I could see my fear looking back at me – it was in the form of darkness. I was then able to smile at my fear without judgment of any kind. It was as if I was waving goodbye to all my fear. My shaman told me that my masculine had run my life, that the divine feminine had been asleep, and it was now awake. I felt the two energies, my divine masculine and feminine, dancing together for the first time. The balance of the two would aid me on my journey. I left my shaman's house feeling light; any denseness I had previously felt was gone. I felt that this gift of lightness was allowing my journey into the unknown to speed up. Not that I felt rushed or in a hurry, actually quite the opposite. I felt that something had been waiting for me to show up, when and where I didn't know.

The experience with my shaman healer seemed to hold the key to balancing my two sides. I learned that my father's looming and large presence in my life wasn't the only problem. My mother hadn't shown up and taken ownership over her empowerment as a woman. God knows she tried – my father just wore her out.

That same day I drove to the attorney's office and signed my final signature on our divorce. It felt like one more step I needed to take. Driving home was a time to listen to my inner voice. I was at peace with everything and, more importantly, I was at peace with myself. I stopped for a late lunch at a café. I walked inside the café and seated myself near a window that overlooked the outside patio. There were a few people eating at the outside tables. A small party of women attracted my attention – one in particular stood out. I was stunned: I was staring at the woman I had a relationship with six years earlier. I hadn't seen her since our swift parting. Of all the days I could have run into her, this day, the day I signed my divorce papers . . . I sat and thought about this. I didn't believe for a second that it was a coincidence. The universe was allowing me to see a painful lesson I had to learn. It was a reminder of the person who spent his whole life lying to himself. The imprint of that moment in time will forever be with me as a loving gentle reminder. I quietly left the café and drove home.

The following week was the week the potential buyers of my business were in town. They seemed very nice; I felt immediately that they would be a good fit, and they must have felt the same way. Before they left town a letter of intent to buy and some earnest money was on the table. We signed the agreement, with ten days as a window for either party to back out. From the day I put my practice up for sale only nine days had gone by and it was under contract. The doors were opening fast. I sat back in awe at the whole process. The East Coast was calling, and the path that I would take was unfolding.

My wife was now becoming extremely close to my parents. My conversations with her were a little strange, there was an undercurrent of anger. I felt that I needed to be very careful what I said to her. Keeping our subject matter focused on the children eased some of the tension. My father had successfully convinced the entire family that I was a full-blown liar. The irony was I hadn't even spoken to any of my family members, with the exception of my sister, who was now on the fringes of support from our family. It was a welcome change for her; she explained to me on many occasions how she needed space from the family. From now on any information I received about my family was filtered through my sister. Most of the information I asked her not to tell me – I didn't want the burden of all the gory details. The blame of no longer speaking to my family was placed directly on my shoulders, I was the one who didn't want to speak to them – as if they were there with open arms. In a way they were exactly right, I did walk away. I felt that I no longer had a choice: either receive their conditional love with all the strings attached, or remove myself from my own family. I had to choose the latter. I was comfortable with the outcome, and the path slowly aligned me with completely letting go. The next chapter in my life would rely heavily on my ability to detach.

My spiritual guides were speaking, I could hear them when I was running, sitting by a river, under a tree, hiking a mountain trail – a voice of wisdom and knowledge whispering across the vast unknown, stretching wide, opening the realm of possibility into all that I am, and all that I am not, stripping away layer upon layer, opening me to authenticity and wonder. It was like a dream that pushed through to the reality I was living. People, places, appeared as gifts in my life. There were no longer any coincidences: everything had its place and purpose. Everyone I met, whether I was running, or eating lunch alone – it all held endless opportunities. Life was now fresh and alive.

I had my children that weekend, we went to a waterslide park. Watching my kids splash around and have fun made me smile. When they were laughing, I was laughing. I coaxed my two oldest girls to go down the larger slide; it took a little effort, but they finally went. I couldn't get them off that slide when it was time to go. The next day we went to another swimming pool. The time I had with them was precious, especially as I knew that I would be leaving soon. I hadn't told my wife any of the details about selling my practice. I wanted to make sure that everything fell into place before breaking the news.

My trip back to visit my friends in New York was now only two weeks away. I was confident that I would make some great connections that might help support my decision to head to the East Coast. Everything else seemed to fall into place so well. I figured making good connections would be the easy part. If someone had told me when I booked my trip to New York that my practice would have already sold, I would never have believed them. It all was happening so fast; all I could do was enjoy the process – I was no longer asking questions. Although leaving my girls was something that loomed large, I felt the way was set. I couldn't walk away from my girls, so I needed to soar for them. I knew they were going to grow up in the same culture and religion I had. Opening their eyes to a different world would be almost impossible, with them living in Utah. So therefore I knew I had to chart my course. There would be a payoff in the future. This was the time to make that happen. I wouldn't let them know of only one way of living. If that was what they chose, then fine; if there was a chance for them to fly at their tender age it had to be through their dad. I would never run from that, after all I had gone through. This would not end with me disappearing.

I woke up early one morning in my little apartment and wrote down the purpose of my life. I knew exactly what it was – I was so sure, I started laughing out loud. It was so obvious, yet so simple. My awakening had a purpose. It was no longer about me. We all have our gifts: my gift was helping others see the beauty that is inside of them. Not my path or my truth – the truth that we all radiate by being our authentic selves. I knew, somehow I just knew that this was my new purpose. I would stay open to however it might manifest in my life. I was certain it would unfold when I was ready.

I couldn't imagine letting go of my profession – all the years in school, student loans, the comfort of a good steady income. But I knew deep within myself that my heart was no longer in my profession. Facing this reality would take time. Something seemed to whisper quietly that it would sort itself out on its own – accepting the outcome was becoming a bit more familiar each day.

When we have accepted ourselves and our current life situations we have appreciation and trust that it is exactly the way it is supposed to be for that moment. We trust in the creativity of how our desires manifest, not with expectations of when and how. It is a simple knowing that we get what we want, just not the way we think it will happen. Life flourishes, creativity happens, flowers bloom, trees grow, healing mends the broken heart, humans evolve. The planet and all life-forms, including humans, exist as one, without conflict, a union within the cycle of life. Everything and everyone expresses that which benefits the whole, not the individual or the idea. Limitations no longer exist; cultural ideas and beliefs fall apart, allowing the limitless whole to continue expanding. We are a part of this process, connected to the whole, whether we are comfortable with it or not. Our very existence this very moment is an expression of total creativity and beauty. The sooner we embrace this the sooner we soar high above the clouds; our view is expanded like that of an eagle, we see everything the way it really is and not the way we have been taught to believe. There is no right or wrong, there are no right answers, we are the answer. The only judgment comes from ourselves. The fact that we exist is one of the greatest expressions of love. We are love – it's at our very core and always will be. As soon as we get out of the way we align with this love. It's always been there. The question is, where have we been?

Chapter 19

The Old Stone Wall

It was nearing the end of June, and I still hadn't heard from anyone in my family. I hadn't really expected to. My father's campaign against me won almost all of his children over. His frustration was spilling over in the direction of my sister: her support of my new life was foiling his plans to have me isolated. From his controlling perspective, alienating his son might somehow bring me back to the fold – in his words, 'come back on his hands and knees asking for forgiveness of his sins'. A broken-down son would serve his beliefs and, of course, his ego. A son that he had rejected, verbally abused, physically abused, lied to. If this son soared away from his nest, it might blow his whole belief structure apart. The unexplainable would not fit well within the Mormon culture. A comfortable sweeping under the rug would be better: 'Your mother and I will only remember the good times and forget all the bad' – again failing to accept the truth while walling out the beautiful energy of healing.

I arrived on a Sunday evening to say goodbye to my girls. Although I would only be gone for one week, I wouldn't see them for almost two weeks. I spent a few hours hanging out with them. Every opportunity I had with our little Kate was delightful; holding her was something I longed for. I kissed and hugged all four of my girls goodbye. I was flying out Tuesday morning with my good friend: we would accompany each other back to New York. I had a little over four weeks left before I actually moved to New York. Where I would be living and where I would work was yet to be determined. I was flying by the seat of my pants, and quite comfortable with this.

As I boarded the plane and sat in my seat, I opened my writing that I had begun almost two weeks ago. My journal writing had now moved to writing a book about my life and the journey I had embarked on. Writing my story was a task that I was willing to start; the question was, how would I see it through. Initially I had an overwhelming urge to spell out my journey as best I could, speaking my truth. The freedom that I now had access to opened as a small paragraph, then a page, then three pages; after three pages I would feel exhausted. When I wrote, I wept with anguish and doubt, struggling to articulate the truth. I became aware of the actual time I was writing about – it was as though I was reliving the entire event. The short sessions while I wrote would explode into a magical moment of creativity and aliveness. It was a process that excited me and at the same time scared the hell out of me. When I went to bed at night, I would be writing in my head – sentences and whole paragraphs would flow. I could no longer stop the flow of words.

We landed in New Jersey: my friend's girlfriend was there to greet us with a smile. We headed to her wooded spread in New York. I was once again reunited with a good spot that felt safe and comfortable. I was eager to make some connections to help ease my transition when I moved out here. The first few nights, we spent some time in the city and met some good people. Then the opportunity to travel to Rhode Island presented itself unexpectedly. I went along for the ride with my friends. It was a part of the country that I hadn't ever seen, and I was more than happy to go on a new adventure. The timing was perfect: Fourth of July weekend. I found myself on this beautiful island where everything was quaint and old world. The landscape was filled with beautiful beaches, jagged rocky cliffs, huge old-style houses, and sailing boats everywhere. It was like I had stepped right into a postcard. My friend's girlfriend introduced us to two of her girlfriends from Boston whom she had planned to spend the weekend with: this was a girls' getaway weekend, and my friend and I had crashed the party. Later in the evening we headed into the small downtown district, where all the bars and pubs were bustling with people. My friend and I went off and left the girls to enjoy their night together.

We spent a good part of the night sitting on a park bench – me smoking a big cigar, my friend puffing away on his favorite pipe. We chatted about our lives, and the culture we found ourselves swimming through. We talked about our Mormon missions and of course our marriages and how they ended. Our paths had been similar but at the same time very different. Mostly we talked about the meaning of life; the role religion had played, good and bad; freedom to explore yourself, freedom to express, freedom to create. It was a good conversation, in a great spot. Seeing the Northeast opened my eyes to the beauty of this vast land we live in, the expanse of trees that go for miles and miles, the density of the forest – it's incredible.

I was becoming acutely aware of good friends and good places, and this was one of those times. Later in the evening we met up with the girls in a bar. It was crowded with so many people you could barely move, and it was difficult to have a conversation of any kind above the loud music. My friend and his girlfriend disappeared into a frenzy of dancing intoxication. One of the other girls from Boston was there with me: there was some kind of connection between us, we were in some way drawn to each other. Through the windows I saw a small pier with some tables and chairs. I felt the urge to go outside and sit by the water alone, somewhere where I could quietly reflect on the experiences I had shared and the places I had seen, and also to think about my girls back in Utah. I told my new friend that I would be outside. She asked me rather matter-of-factly, 'Are you gay?' I started laughing. It was the first time in my life I had ever been asked this question; I took it as a compliment in a strange sort of way. After I stopped laughing I told her, 'No I am not gay.' My thoughts turned to my shaman healer back in Utah. She had told me, after all, that she had awoken my feminine side. That thought caused me to laugh even more – I couldn't stop. I wondered what in the world my shaman had done to me.

The next day was the Fourth of July. We spent nearly the whole day at the beach. I ran through the waves like a child, we played frisbee; it was a great day. That evening my new friend and I stood next to a stone wall that looked well over two hundred years old and watched the fireworks explode over the Atlantic Ocean. It was a memorable moment for me. Her culture and mine were glaringly different, but I enjoyed the time we spent together. The girls once again disappeared into the night, and my childhood friend and I found ourselves sitting on that same stone wall, blowing smoke into the cool night air. It came to me in that moment that the nightlife scene wasn't for me. Sitting on a quiet deck somewhere close to nature, sharing a bottle of wine with good friends, sounded just about perfect. I spoke with my daughters that evening, sitting on the same stone wall – I heard all about their experiences, the fireworks they had seen, and the pet frogs they took home. I was happy that night to share three lovely moments with that old stone wall: my girls, my childhood friend and my new friend from Boston.

We took our time leaving this quaint little island. The two girls from Boston said their goodbyes, and my friend and his girlfriend went for a cliff walk. I stayed behind to write, sitting by the beach, with my sunglasses on and my hat pulled low. My quiet reflection over my childhood years brought some unexpected emotions to the surface. I cried and cried – I didn't even care if anyone noticed. It was an emotional release I badly needed. Afterwards, the lightness in my step returned, the cool ocean breeze felt good against my sunburned body. It felt as though the shift in energy joined with the energy of the ocean. The union seemed to flow through my soul, a gentle reminder that my wounds were healing. I smiled at the ocean and thanked the mother of creation, and this beautiful universe we are all so much a part of.

The drive back to New York was just as beautiful as the drive there. My moment of truth was approaching. How it would all unfold? It didn't really matter anymore, I trusted the expanse of the universe, my wounds were healing – it doesn't get any better than that. What more did I need? I had no expectations, no limitations. My good friend dropped me off at the airport Tuesday afternoon and we said our goodbyes. It seemed that his time on the East Coast was winding down, he intended to pack up soon and head back to Utah. I had thought he would be on the East Coast when I moved there, but it wasn't to be. I allowed it to be exactly that, it was supposed to happen this way. We joked about my drive out to the East Coast and his drive back west, and how we could high five in Iowa. We had a good laugh over that one.

Chapter 20

Dragonflies, Resignation, Gardens and Nature

As soon as I got back to Utah I knew that it would be a flurry of activity. The new owners would be in my practice. We had set aside three weeks for a transition with the patients, after which I would leave them the key, load my few belongings into my car and make the long drive. The reality of my new life was sinking in. I had my children for the upcoming weekend, and had promised them we would pitch a tent at the campground next door to the waterslide park. I picked them up on a Thursday night and we loaded up the tent and all their sleeping bags. They were full of excitement and of course so was I. I wanted to enjoy as much time with my girls as possible before I left. I had talked to them about the possibility of me leaving, though I hadn't yet told them the exact date. It was a subject that they hated; I had to tread lightly, but I wanted to be honest and upfront with them.

The next day we had a great time. I went down the waterslide with my girls at least a dozen times. I felt like a ten-year-old all over again – it was wonderful to connect with them in such a childlike way. We pitched the tent and as soon as it got dark we lay side by side in our sleeping bags. The girls were like any young kids their age, giggling and kicking their legs, screaming, laughing, and I was laughing right along with them. The next day we went to a dinosaur park. Watching my girls run and jump was something I used to take for granted; I never noticed little things like that. I would arrive home from work and plop myself down in front of the TV. I hate to admit it, but I traded many moments I could have been more present for my girls because of being preoccupied with nothing of any importance. I could not see the value of sitting in the grass while watching them play after a long day of work. Now my time with them was precious, and I wanted to squeeze every little emotion into a single day. It was like I was seeing them for the first time: I watched their every move, I treasured their creativity and aliveness. My heart ached when I thought of leaving them. I vowed that I would return as often as I could, and I reminded myself that it was only a five-hour flight. There were other quiet moments when I questioned what the hell I was doing – the moments of doubt overwhelmed me at times.

I had less than three weeks before my departure. My writing continued, although very slowly. I dropped my girls off on Sunday morning, took my running gear and went to my favorite little trail. It is shaded in the trees for most of the run, right along the lake. Feeling loneliness and some doubt, I headed off. In the last mile of my run a little bird flew right over my shoulder. His body was golden yellow, with black wings. I had never seen such a beautiful little bird before. He flew back again immediately over my left shoulder. It was like he was speaking to me. He disappeared for a moment, then there he was again, following me. Once again he ducked out of sight, then back again, tweet, tweet, he was full of enchanting music. He disappeared one last time; I didn't see him for a couple of hundred yards. As I finished my run there he was, flying right over me: he flew a few circles then disappeared. I had the distinct impression that this beautiful little bird was assuring me I was on the right path, everything would work out in the end, I was going where I needed to go.

I couldn't help but think of all the little signs and clues I had overlooked throughout my life. It didn't matter now, because now I wasn't missing anything. If we are willing to look, nature will guide us in a gentle loving direction. I sent off my application for licensure in the state of New Jersey: I intended to get my license and follow up with the chiropractor I had met. My living arrangements fell into place just in time. My good friend had already returned to Utah, and his girlfriend kindly offered me the guestroom in her house for as long as I needed. I was grateful, and once again I was astonished at the way everything fell into place. It was as though the wind had gently blown me in an easterly direction. Friends and patients would ask me, 'Why the East Coast, what's out there?' I would simply reply 'The wind is blowing me in that direction.' I would continue to write my story, that I was sure of. With space and honesty my pen would flow.

I had only a few more doors to close so that new ones could open. I told my wife that weekend when I was leaving. I don't think she was at all surprised. She did ask, 'Why so soon?' The only answer I could give is the one I just wrote. I didn't expect her or anyone else to understand. Within a few days my wife's anger seemed to melt away. She gave me what support she could. She said, 'I know this is something you have to do.' This unexpected moment of loving support was like witnessing a miracle. I drove away that day with tears in my eyes.

In those tender moments of forgiveness and acceptance there is a stillness that stirs the soul. Grace is the surrender to life unfolding on its own, without expectation or control, feeling each situation as though it was always of our choosing. Everything in that moment becomes one, because the struggle for this or that is no longer attached to a specific outcome. A feeling of lightness frees us from the heaviness of plans and deadlines. We can show up with agility and flexibility without worry of a distraction or obstacle getting in our way. Because all of that would have meaning to our journey and make it even more special. Creativity naturally thrives when we spontaneously act rather than reacting to outside influences. Being connected to the rhythm of nature, the trees, the wind, the birds, rustling leaves, was always a reminder of this moment being the only one that mattered.

I was once again on a run. This time I had a dragonfly that followed me almost the entire way – if I reached out I could almost touch it. The grace with which a dragonfly moves is delicately woven between flying and dancing; it is beauty in motion. I was so moved by my little friend that as soon as I got home I looked up the spiritual meaning of a dragonfly. Here is what I found in Chris Luttichau's book, *Animal Spirit Guides*:

> Dragonfly encourages us to see the illusions that define us. Let him guide you to the forgotten part of your soul, so that an understanding of your true self can begin to emerge . . . Realizing our true potential, in a way that also benefits other people, is the ultimate expression of the power of the dragonfly.

I was absolutely fascinated by this – it mirrored my own life almost exactly.

The time had arrived for me to remove my name from the Mormon Church and officially step away from an institution that no longer served me. I had no bad feelings of any kind towards them, but I no longer felt it was necessary to have my name on their records. The lack of tolerance and the division I had experienced were something I needed to walk away from. I had waited a few years to make it official, but after the ending of my marriage I knew it was only a matter of time. For some reason I felt the need to have my name removed before I headed to the East Coast. I had been told that it could be a difficult process – the church would rather excommunicate you than allow you to resign. Here is a copy of a letter I found on exmormon.com. I typed it up and sent it to the church headquarters, certified mail.

> This letter is my formal resignation from the Church of Jesus Christ of Latter-day Saints and it is effective immediately. I hereby withdraw my consent to being treated as a member and I withdraw my consent to being subject to church rules, policies, beliefs and discipline. As I am no longer a member, I want my name permanently and completely removed from the membership rolls of the church. I have given this matter considerable thought. I understand what you consider the seriousness and the consequences of my actions. I am aware that the Church handbook says that my resignation 'cancels the effects of baptism and confirmation, withdraws the priesthood and revokes temple blessings.' My resignation should be processed immediately, without any

waiting periods. I am not going to be dissuaded and I'm not going to change my mind. I expect this matter to be handled promptly, with respect and with full confidentiality. After today, the only contact I want from the church is a single letter of confirmation to let me know that I am no longer listed a member of the church.

I felt like celebrating when I sent in my letter: the day had finally arrived. They could do whatever the hell they wanted; as far as I was concerned I was no longer a Mormon. Their long arm of control was severed that day.

It had been a long journey, overwhelming at times. The family, the church all blended into one unit that saw things only in black and white, weaving a pattern of division. Their banner of truth and the call to serve their God are written in their book, the book they claim holds all truth. It is a fable so divisive that the Book of Mormon leaves only one man standing. After a thousand-year history of two warring factions, the side that wins the battle is always the side that is following God's plan the best. When both sides stop following God, thousands slaughter each other with one remaining survivor. This man is left with the responsibility to hide away handed-down records on gold plates to save the historical period from being lost.

Is it any wonder that a tale spun under such illusion would travel the same path of destruction today? Mormons believe that the better you follow all the rules, the more God will bless you with money. This is the clear message in the Book of Mormon. Keep God's commandments and you will become a wealthy nation, with gold and silver. Their holy scripture sums up the quest that the Mormons are on: the blind leading the blind. Money is more important than people, because money buys image. If image wasn't important to the Mormons then why are billions of dollars spent on temples – superficial structures dripping with gold and silver? It is a religious cult that has become the embodiment of materialism, all in the name of God. Division is caused by greed, with a suffocating black-and-white doctrine that all truth is owned by the Mormon Church.

The manicured garden might best describe my religious roots. The manicured garden is beautiful, it is set out in rows. Curbing and clipping need the hand of the gardener; maintenance is required for the garden to flourish. The maintained garden appears as the only source of beauty. If the flower stepped outside of its uniformed row the gardener would replace the flower as though it had overstepped its boundaries. Flowering would no longer exist within the tapestry of the whole. The gardener would appear empty-handed, once again looking to the perception of the mind. The garden could only be its gardener's inclusive illusion of beauty.

Nature, on the other hand, wouldn't allow boundaries of cement edging. Nature fulfills its boundless state of existence without control. Nature's expanse of endless growth captures an awakening of freedom, the freedom to explore the evolution of life expanding in any direction. The art of growth and finding natural beauty is when control is removed, expectations are left out. Then growth flourishes, abundantly displaying an array of color that leaves the observer in awe.

I was leaving the manicured garden, without judgment – such gardens have their own beauty. For me, it was time to embrace the vast landscape I found in nature: here was the rhythm I felt that aligned perfectly with spirituality.

Chapter 21

Dragonfly Healing, Soaring from the Nest

The upcoming weekend was my last with my girls before driving to the East Coast. By now they knew when I would be leaving, but it was still a tough subject to talk about with them. On a quiet drive around the lake, nine-year-old Chloe tentatively told me that she had a dream. In her dream she was flying high above the clouds. I told her that I used to have the same dreams when I was a little boy. I explained to her that she could really fly. She was surprised at my response. 'How can I really fly?' she asked me. I told her, 'Never listen to anyone who tells you what you are or what you can become. Explore your own possibilities; don't let anybody tell you what you can be in life. You will fly high above the clouds in your own creative way.' I had captured her childlike expression of being completely free. I continued, 'Jump off the cliff and you will soar. Dive down and explore the ocean floor, rise to the surface, break out of the water and fly high over the cliffs of your imagination. Fly over the expanse of the Rocky Mountains. Take in the awe of this beautiful globe we are so much a part of. Land softly in a field of wildflowers, smile at the beauty, it will smile back. Keep soaring, my darling Chloe, you will reach high, your journey will be exactly that. There will be people who don't want you to fly; fly anyway.' We made a little pact that day that we are flyers together, we can always fly. 'Believe it,' I told her. 'Find the answer within you.'

Shortly before I left, I booked two different trips. One trip seemed a little surreal: a flight from New York to Salt Lake City five weeks after my arrival. I wanted my girls to know exactly when I would be back. The other trip was spontaneous but felt perfect. I hadn't been to New Zealand in twenty years. It was time to return, to connect once again with my extended family. My journey had brought me full circle in so many ways. I booked this trip over Thanksgiving week, knowing that my wife would be spending Thanksgiving with the kids and of course her family. My family, on the other hand – that was a story that would continue to unfold. My hope would always be that the rest of my family would be able to heal; but for healing to happen, there first needs to be acceptance of what has happened, taking responsibility for our actions.

The next five to six days would present moments that felt almost insurmountable. What I had signed up for was so fresh and new that the twists and turns would leave me reeling with emotional doubts, tumbling along in a freefall.

On my way to say a final goodbye to my children, I stopped to get a cup of coffee at a small coffee shop. A very attractive woman was making my latte. We started talking – small talk at first, which quickly turned to my life and the journey I had been on, and the one I was about to embark on. She asked, 'Are you doing okay?' Taking a deep breath I said, 'I think so, we will soon see.' She told me that she was a shaman healer: that got my full attention. I felt that perhaps she could help me somehow, before I left. She handed me her card and told me to call her later that evening; she could maybe arrange to meet with me the next day. I thanked her and left. As I was driving away, I took her card out and looked at it. To my surprise, the background image was a large green dragonfly. I knew then that I would call her later that evening. The universe was pointing me in the direction of a dragonfly healer. The significance of my not-so-chance meeting would be extremely valuable in the week to follow.

I spent the rest of my morning with my girls, and I got some great pictures with them. It seemed like any summer day, being there with them. My ex-wife was understanding and supportive. She actually said that she was attempting to distance herself from my family, though whether that was true or not I had no way of knowing. I waved goodbye to my ex-wife and my daughters. I wondered how I would fare over the course of the next month, not seeing my girls – but it was an experience that I was willing to face. Ironically, I had to do it for them: I had to leave my girls in order to fully be there for them. Somehow I felt that it would only be temporary, and this whispering thought brought some comfort. The journey teaches us exactly that, we are so much more than we ever thought possible. One step, another step and then another, then we are walking, then we are running, all of a sudden we are flying, reaching heights that were once so far out of reach, we thought they were only a dream.

That evening I called my new shaman friend. We arranged to meet next to the lake in the early afternoon the following day. She told me that nature was her office: I knew I was in good hands. Missing my appointment with her wouldn't happen in a million years. I did not know what to expect – I would allow it to be exactly what it was supposed to be.

The next morning I officially handed over my business to the new owners. Leaving my key behind was a strange feeling – I thought to myself, I just left a rather large, steady income. Walking away from that last safety net was frightening. I felt a freedom I hadn't felt in years.

We met that afternoon at a little spot right next to the water. I noticed a silver dragonfly dangling around her neck. We sat down and talked for maybe twenty minutes. We talked about the culture, the breakup of my marriage, the journey I was about to embark on. I lay down close to the water's edge. The water was calm. I could hear a few boats in the distance, the sound of children being pulled on a tube. I closed my eyes and allowed my body to drift in the direction of healing. It felt as though I was drifting between two realms of consciousness – the dream state to nothing. Time stood still, as though there was no time. I felt suspended between my perception of reality and no reality. The feeling of lightness pervaded my entire existence. Afterwards my shaman told me, whatever support I may feel has deserted me here, on the other side I had more support. The angels had amassed around me. I wasn't alone on my journey. She sent me away with a small green stone and a little figure of a man. The meaning of both I had no idea, but I knew that both items would accompany me on my journey.

I met up with my childhood friend soon after my shaman experience. We spent our time together sitting in a dried-up creek bed. I had my new whittling knife and a large stick I had found on a long hike with a friend. I was finishing removing the top layer of bark, it was therapy for me. Drinking a beer together in the middle of nature felt about as perfect as our imperfect lives had been. Comforting each other with a few laughs over the imperfections was the best part. We talked about my family and how they now believed I was crazy. They had declared that I had lost my mind. Ironically, they were right, I had lost my mind – it seemed to be a prerequisite for my journey.

Dropping my friend off felt like another chapter in my life had closed. I was beginning a fresh chapter where I would have the opportunity to be alone for a few months, the time to quietly sit in nature learning the silent language of the universe – not a voice filled with words, rather a melody of different sounds and vibrations that one can hear every day with open eyes and ears. I drove to my sister's house, where she and her family would share dinner with me. I had written a letter to my mother that I wanted to leave with my sister. I knew that she would give it to her at the right time. Here is what I wrote to her.

Dear Mom

I am writing this letter to let you know that I love you. You have been a great mother to me. I understand the difficulty of your position. It's almost like you have to choose a side in our family. Going through perhaps one of the most difficult challenges of my life, my own family deserted me. I understand you may not see it this way, that's okay, being told by my own father that I am a failure in front of my daughters, was the end of that path for me. The control and fear that I have been raised with has a heavy price. I don't blame anyone, or the church for that matter. It has simply been my life's lessons I accept these lessons with gratitude in my heart. I would not be who I am today without these lessons. I made a very conscious decision to face the truth in my own life. I understand that facing the truth can be a painful journey, I am living this truth. Henry David Thoreau wrote 'I would have each one be very careful to find out and pursue

his own way, and not his father's or his mothers or his neighbors.' So therefore I feel that I must pursue my own path. We each have our own version of truth I have found mine it has been inside me the whole time. I love my children and my wife for that matter, it has broken my heart to leave them in this way however I will create a different life for them, new possibilities. So for now I must break away from the tribe, family, culture, comforts. I go to live my truth. I hope you can find it in your soul to accept my undertaking. I will stay in the moment this is where I find peace.
Lots of love, your son

I enjoyed the time I spent that last evening with my sister. We talked about the family and all the crazy events that had occurred over the last four months. I felt relieved that I had gotten through most of the craziness; there were definitely times I didn't think I would make it.

The next morning I went to my old business to gather anything I might have left behind and to say goodbye to the new owners and wish them luck. While I was there I received a letter from the church records division, which had just arrived in the mail. I was eager for confirmation that my name had been removed; but this wasn't the case.

Dear Brother Preston:
I have been asked to acknowledge your recent letter in which you request that your name be removed from the membership records of the Church of Jesus Christ of Latter-day Saints. I have also been asked to inform you that the church considers such a request to be an ecclesiastical matter that must be handled by local priesthood leaders before being processed by Church employees. Therefore, your letter and a copy of this reply are being sent to your local church leaders. Your bishop will contact you concerning the fulfillment of your request. In view of the eternal consequences of such an action, the brethren urge you to reconsider your request and to prayerfully consider the enclosed statement of the first presidency.

I smiled to myself at the control and their inability to just let people leave on their own accord. It was a reminder of what I had walked away from. I was mostly grateful that I had let go of it emotionally. I felt that for those that wanted to participate, wonderful, enjoy your membership – it's fine, it's okay. Please just allow those who want to leave, to leave with some individual dignity and respect. The arrogant assumption that you can no longer be happy without the church was cause for serious reflection. Their way of living isn't for everyone. I know that they see it differently, but the point was simply that. I knew it was no longer a battle between good and evil: the laying down of the ego was the only thing that made sense to me. That was exactly my new position: I no longer needed to have an ego. I gathered the last of my things together and left my old identity behind in a place I used to call mine.

I spent the next two hours at my little apartment, loading my clothes and other personal belongings into my car. I had given away all of my books except my cherished favorites, all fifteen books I would need on my journey. The last thing I put in my car was my journal and two empty ones – I knew that my writing would continue. I stood by my loaded-down car while my landlady friend took my picture. I didn't want to miss anything, my journey was only beginning. We hugged, said the usual goodbyes. As I drove out of town I thought to myself, 'Good god, I really am doing this?' I smiled and turned the music up to my new theme song, 'Freedom', by Akon.

I had twenty-five hundred miles to drive; I'd better get comfortable. I aimed my car in the direction of the Colorado Mountains. I had a good friend who was staying in a resort town there, exhibiting her beautiful paintings. I thought that it would be a good spot to land on my first night.

Chapter 22

Dying and Living

My first day of driving was relaxing and fairly easy. It felt good to follow through with my journey. There were a few moments of doubt, but nothing of any real significance. I found the little resort town at about ten o'clock that night. It helped to have a friend greet me at the end of my first day of driving. The following morning I pulled on my running shoes and headed out the door. I was amazed at how beautiful it was, nestled in the mountains at nine thousand feet above sea level. It was like something you would see in a magazine. My run was anything but flat, breathing the thin air, it felt like I hadn't run in months; but the beauty of the mountainous surroundings made up for the lack of oxygen. After my run, I showered and made my way into the ski village. It was bustling with artists setting up their displays, booths with paintings of all kinds of life, sculptures of bronze and wood. Some of the artists were even busily in the act of painting. I soon found my friend, and she showed me her impressive display of paintings. Her artistic ability brought the beauty of trees to life in a way that seemed to capture their very essence.

I made my way up to the chairlifts and gondola, and found a quiet table to sit at with a panoramic view of the whole mountainside. Children were running and jumping; their excited screams and cheering filled me with a sense of longing for my girls back home. My emotions felt fresh and fragile hearing all of the children. I smiled at the families that paraded by. I thought to myself, that used to be me. I surrendered to the fact that it wasn't, allowed my emotions instead to turn to appreciation. I pulled out my journal, putting pen to paper. The gratitude I felt in my heart allowed my story to flow.

I awoke early next morning, threw on my running shoes and enjoyed a comfortable run. I knew the day ahead would be lonely and long. I gathered my few belongings, said goodbye to my artist friend and her daughter, thanked them for their hospitality. As I left the mountain sanctuary behind I pondered the beauty of life, the painful lessons, the opportunity of each lesson that plays itself out on the canvas of our lives. How much we miss throughout our hurried lives. My new journey seemed to slow everything down, bringing everything into intense color and splendor. My senses were alive, yet I felt calm as I drew in the reflection of the mountains and the tall pine trees, mountain streams and lakes. I was leaving it behind – for rows and rows of corn.

I logged almost eight hundred miles that day. The flood of emotions was overwhelming at times. I played a CD over and over – one my sister had given me before I left. It was the sounds of an East Indian vocalist; her voice struck a chord with the sound of love and freedom. It was a nicely timed gift. I pulled in to a clean city in Iowa that seemed like a good spot after a long day of travel. I felt happy with the distance I had driven. I was still riding the waves of excitement of the new adventure I was on. Fear of failure and isolation hadn't really arrived yet, although I had fleeting moments when I had glimpsed them. Being swallowed up by these emotions was still on the horizon. My life on the East Coast would hopefully open up the way I had envisioned. I had a handful of good contacts, and the chiropractic path seemed easy enough – I knew that path well.

The next morning I left with a tinge of doubt that gradually grew and threatened to overwhelm me. I was nervous, but managed to keep my emotions intact. Driving through Iowa was a beautiful display of open cornfields and expansive farms, all with the same barn, it seemed. The cornfields would continue through four states, and the trees would grow more dense as I continued east. I spoke with my sister that Sunday morning while driving through Iowa. Talking with her helped to temporarily calm my turbulent mixture of emotions. The state I was in is difficult to describe – like a loss of control on the emotional level, manifesting subtly on a physical level. I was only just managing to keep it together.

I reached Illinois: I had driven maybe three hundred miles. My emotional world was closing in all around me. I thought a few times that I might have to pull over on the side of the interstate and lay in the abyss of my spiraling collapse. I called the one person who came to mind, my dragonfly healer. She was amazing in her ability to calm the troubled waters. She stayed with me for almost thirty minutes. It was an intense conversation. My new friend helped pull me out of a very tough spot, she was like a midwife that day. She helped me call in my angelic ancestral support. The moment was immediately transformed from thoughts of dying, to elation and overwhelming comfort. I cried. I asked, What the fuck is happening to me? My dragonfly healer assured me it was all normal. I felt that she saved my life that day. My little dragonfly had led me to a place of destiny on my run just a few weeks earlier – thank god that I had been aware of the small signs. I managed to make it to Central North Indiana that day – I had driven four hundred and fifty miles. I found a place to stay in the late afternoon, a place to rest my fragile, rundown body. I was spent. I knew that I would not give up that day, but it was a close call. The best part was my awareness of the emotional void: I wasn't running from those emotions anymore, I was facing them head-on. I would quickly learn that a moment of suffering and being with the intensity of that emotion beats the hell out of suffering in quiet retreat your whole life.

I spent the quiet Sunday evening in a remote Indiana hotel. A large gathering of families and young teenage girls had chosen the same hotel. I later learned they were there for a championship softball tournament. I watched in the large open foyer all of the interaction between each family member. They were passing around pizza that had just been delivered. I couldn't help but think of my own family that I was once so much a part of. Breaking away was not easy – the agony of the old familiar was all around me. The way forward and the ability to be still would save me from my old self asserting itself back into my life. I reflected that the path I was on required solitude and isolation – these qualities would be necessary for a full and honest evaluation of myself. As my thoughts rested, I could comfortably enjoy the moment. I fell into a peaceful sleep that night, with my small green stone clutched in my right hand; it was still there when I awoke in the morning.

It was a brand new day, and I felt much better. I was thankful knowing that I would arrive at my destination that evening. I was even more thankful that I would be staying with a friend, my childhood friend's girlfriend. Seeing a familiar loving face at the end of a long road trip felt reassuring and welcoming. I calculated the final leg: I had seven hundred miles to drive. As I left Indiana, navigated my way through Ohio and entered Pennsylvania, the cornfields were replaced by an impressive landscape of trees, rolling hills and small mountains. I drove through the most beautiful state I had ever seen. The dense expanse of forest went as far as the eye could see. My destination was close, I could feel it. The direction my journey would go was yet to be determined, but I was confident of one thing: I would stay open to all possibilities. Limiting my new life felt old and tiresome.

I could merge into the flow of life, like a gentle river that weaves its path effortlessly over and around the rocks, creating new shapes and dimensions in its exchange, blissfully humming its watery melody, blending in with the sounds of life, giving and receiving, its coolness refreshing its environment constant and steady. No thoughts of yesterday or tomorrow, only awareness of its union with the one source that gives to us all. The lessons from nature would ease the expanse of the unknown for me. Being one with the river allowed the path to unfold the way it was designed.

Chapter 23

Embracing the Unknown

As I neared my new friend's home I was filled with anticipation and excitement. The familiarity of her wooded slice of heaven seemed to draw me in after five days of traveling alone, the people I had met, the changing landscape, the miles I had driven. It was a perfect match for the array of emotions that I had experienced, all of it swirled around in my head. I would soon find out why the universe had hand-delivered me effortlessly to this eastern location. As I pulled into the driveway my heart sang out in overwhelming relief. I stepped out of my car, found a spot on the grass and lay down. I had survived. The freefall at times seemed impossible to control, and it all culminated in that moment. I laughed and cried. Once again the mother of creation embraced my soul. I felt that I was where I was supposed to be. Seeing my friend was comforting, a glowing reminder of good friends and good places. The universe seemed to know the exact moment for the right people to show up in my life.

It had only been four months since my first visit to my friend's house; now here I was living for an indefinite amount of time. The next day, I busied myself with finalizing my chiropractic licensure in the state of New Jersey. I left messages with half a dozen contacts that seemed promising. My networking ability in times past had opened many doors and here I felt that, with some effort, my network would grow. I found myself knocking on empty doors; no one returned any of my messages. I was surprised, as some of my contacts were really solid. I knew my heart was no longer in my profession. Was it time to fully walk away from something I once believed was the only thing for me?

It seemed as though a giant curtain had wrapped itself around my new life. My inner voice spoke to me:

> It was our job to get you here, this exact location; we have been waiting for you to arrive. Do what inspires and empowers you, create the beauty you see in yourself and in everyone around you. Write for them, empower others to find their voice, it's your personal calling. Through the unfolding of your personal calling others will find their personal calling. Your message will resonate with some; they will resonate with others. Your ripple on the open water will cause other ripples that will create even more ripples of conscious awakening. This is your purpose; it is why we are all here, to create peace, love, harmony, it's who we are. It's our personal calling to radiate who we are, the essence of all things beautiful.

My purpose now became clear to me: I would finish writing my life story. I wouldn't stop writing until my inner voice spoke to my heart. The alone time, the isolation would capture my soul. I immersed myself in nature, I listened to what it had to say. I was learning the language of my soul. Through it all my story would spill onto blank pages. My pen became my instrument of personal healing and creativity; I was alive, alert.

The next morning I was reunited with an old friend, my seven-mile country run. I greeted every hill and corner with an embrace of gratitude for the connectivity of all living things. I was thankful for the source we are all connected to. As I rounded the last left-hand bend to my amazement right, in front of me, fifteen to twenty gold and black-winged little birds burst out of a small tree and flew right over my head. All the way from the west to the east on a simple run, my golden-feathered friends were greeting me with a warm embrace. I thanked them, smiled and laughed. I was on the right path: what more did I need, I was so happy I followed the path. I had been led and reassured by a beautiful golden flock of little birds and comforted by the delicate dancing dragonfly.

The signs along the way helped to calm the many doubts I had. My angels would whisper, *Keep writing, don't stop, just keep writing.* After writing for hours I would feel, okay, I can do this; it was when I quit writing that the doubt would creep in. Everything seemed to have turned upside down. The strange part is, I was okay with it all, I was finally living.

I was living for the first time without a job, without any identity within a community, just doing exactly what gave me joy. I felt raw and exposed. Nature became my long-awaited friend. I realized that the stripping away of all my perceived safety nets opened the door to a horizon that painted beauty and wonder. I craved to have my feet rest on the earth, like we were connecting again, like old friends embracing after many years of separation. I fed on the energy of my life reuniting with one life, the existence of which remained still and unchanged. My journey delivered me into its welcoming arms, whispering, welcome back. The cycle of creativity expanded my old version into new realms of possibility. Observing the creativity of my natural surroundings set fire to the creative life that I was. Falling in love with this creative cycle expanded my destiny to awaken the beauty in everyone and everything. The universe and I were one. The experience caused an unearthing effortless gratitude to erupt in all directions. My spirit soared in appreciation of my union with all living things. I could sit by a small stream and hear its delicious melody. I could hear the wind gently awakening life. The birds sang melodies to my healing heart. As the sun set, the crickets would display a symphony of steady harmonic beauty. The price of admission was free; my new friends asked for nothing back, only giving constantly, gifts of such divine expression in whose chorus springs an everlasting peace, harmony and union where separation and division become extinct.

I was emerging from the depths of despair, alert, awake, drinking in the delicate flow of safe passage, alone but never alone. Feeling an array of emotions without calling any of them good or bad. Seeing my whole life through a lens that only visualized truth, with no judgment of this part or that part. I could finally see how I had tried to keep up this perfect image, when letting go and accepting myself as human was the ultimate reward and act of freedom. I had finally succeeded in honoring the most important opinion: the opinion I had of myself. I had nothing in the material sense, but I didn't care, I felt what I had discovered was worth more than all the money in the world.

At times the cultural conditioning would reawaken my fears and doubts. I would observe the life that I was living and the life I had left behind. I was comfortable with my new surroundings; better yet, I was embracing the alone with quiet abandonment. What previously seemed daunting because of my once fear-stricken existence was now easy. This stream of brilliant bliss broke every barrier that had previously held me prisoner. Letting go of everything became a natural reflex aimed at weightless flight. Soaring with nature gave me confidence to trust its unconditional embrace. Finding solace with a wounded heart allowed my walls to crumble inward. My loving friend would never leave me. I was in touch with life itself, greeting me from a long journey; the desert was no more.

My daughters back home would at times weigh heavy on my broken heart. Hearing their voices would bring solace, but I still longed for their embrace. Comforting them across the geographical separation at times was difficult.

The pen continued weaving healing and honesty along my journey. My former illusion of the grand scheme of family life and career had left me bereft and full of wonder. My newfound ability to embrace the present moment left me floating in quiet solitude. My new location on the East Coast was perfect for now, but I knew that it would not become my home. The world seemed an expanse of isolation and separation. I walked the landscape of the East Coast in quiet retreat from my former life. Returning was no longer possible; the doors had closed. I was no longer interested in anything that required a specific answer, because no one knows the answer. I had chosen to let go of wanting or waiting for the truth to arrive like a sign from God. The moment magically arrived with knowing that truth resides inside – not in any religion or any outside structure.

The new discussions that floated around family and community were that I was losing my mind; I had once again gone crazy. This news was filtered through my only sibling whose support was steadfast – my sister. Her support and genuine love for me hammered the last nail in her coffin from the family, who saw her love for me as an act of betrayal. The family was in the grip of a single-minded monopoly, led by a doctrine so black and white that they would draw a sword rather than seek peace and resolution. Her hand in Christ-like gesture towards the outcast son, ironically, alienated her further from the family that was hell-bent on mouthing that Christ is their savior. This seemed a far cry from the Christian message of the man they embrace, the one they hold dear. To them it was a conflict between right and wrong: whose side are you on? But the Christ I remember never took sides. Was the division of family and marriage a war that Jesus would have watched, triumphantly waving a flag for his team? This seems so contrary to his very nature. For my family, though, the path to eternal life seemed to justify the exclusion of life itself.

The way I see it, if life itself was created by a higher being, wouldn't our very existence be enough for unconditional love? We are all adored just by the simple fact that we exist: our very existence is evidence that we are love.

Chapter 24

Shattering Former Limitations

I placed a chair underneath a grove of massive trees; they hung over me in a warm embrace. The solitude and connectivity to the Earth allowed my writing to expand in a way I had never dreamed possible: hours would go by as if it had only been one hour. My quiet retreat opened the doorway into the present, connecting me with an intelligence that spoke a language I was only beginning to understand. I allowed myself to follow the energetic flow; stepping outside of this new language wasn't possible. I was swept into the calm, creative flow that was all around me. The more I wrote the more familiar I became with this universal language. At times I would stop writing, observe my surroundings and feel the inner aliveness of the moment. I was at one with the process, there was no stress; actually quite the opposite.

The abuse and shadows of the past unfolded magically into forgiveness and love; no longer was there any blame. It felt liberating to write the truth for the first time about the abuse that had been in the family for generations. It became clear that the abuser felt ashamed by the abuse that happened to them – not only shame but anger, without accepting where the anger was coming from. The abuser knows the truth deep down but is afraid to acknowledge it, so uses anger and control to cover what they are afraid to accept. Shame leads the way into a dark tunnel of more abuse – why? Out of fear of what others may think of them. The abuser doesn't realize that the truth lies within, a voice of power and conviction to accept what is and take a truthful stand to say, 'I need help and I no longer want to abuse anyone; even more, I no longer want to abuse myself.'

Not wanting anyone to know what you have gone through builds a wall of denial that temporarily feels safe. When safety aids denial it becomes a slippery slope of make-believe that what happened never happened – a dangerous place to be if you no longer want to repeat abuse. The only way to distance myself from the horrors of physical abuse was by facing it head-on, accepting it – not from a perspective of blame but as a vision of rising above any victimhood, taking a role in changing past behavior. My mission now is to be a light within myself; and to heal and aid others in seeing this light within themselves.

My return to Salt Lake City was a trip that I anxiously awaited, knowing that my girls would be eager to see me, and I them. My childhood friend was there to pick me up. As we traveled to the little valley in the mountains, I reflected over the last month. It had been an intense, beautiful, creative experience. My isolation, though, had left little room for me to contemplate my love for my children. Seeing my daughters again was the focus of this trip; and my time with them would be special and precious. Reconnecting with my girls expanded my vision to follow the path of self-discovery. I realized the time of separation from them had allowed a whole world to open, like a river of renewed beauty. My return to the safety of the familiar shattered my former belief that safety had ever been here. My experience, I would not have traded for all the money in the world. During that time, a whole new level of creativity I had never known was born. I welcomed the knowledge that limitation only lives within the confines of the mind. I could experience such beauty, aligned with nature: how could it happen any other way? We are all the same energy of creativity – imagine the beauty we could create if all living things connected and resonated with respect and acceptance.

The next day I arrived at my kids' school to eat lunch with them in the cafeteria. I ate first with Sophie; to my delight she swallowed me up into her arms the moment she saw me. I was the king of her little world. Watching her with her friends was the best part. I couldn't take my eyes off my daughter. I thought how, two years earlier, I never would have been there. I then had the opportunity to eat lunch with Chloe who, as a fourth grader, was more reserved, hanging back in innocent embarrassment at her dad's presence. I soon learned to act as though I wasn't there – I simply was her quiet hero. I was more than up for the part. My sixth-grade daughter Maryn gave me a hug and told me lovingly I wasn't welcome at lunch – and I smiled at her grown-up nature. Her new ability to mother little Kate expanded my heart in all directions; she could do no wrong. Her quiet strength reminded me of her independent spirit. Her watchful eye was on her mother and little Kate. I quietly thanked the gods for my oldest daughter Maryn.

Over the following weekend, the activities seemed endless: rock climbing, movies, dinner, picking out small gifts to remember our time together. The stream of activities filled my heart with joy. My pace slowed to almost a standstill as I watched their every move. They were so alive it was breathtaking. Did it take a divorce to open my senses to the presence of my girls? I was at a loss for words to express the newness of it all, the splendor. Pondering why felt meaningless: they were with me, and we were together.

Chapter 25

Forgiveness with Both Hands Wide Open

The cycle of time seems to spin its delicate tapestry into our souls, opening the beauty that was there all along. The shifting sands of time fall like ghosts from a faraway dream. Illusions like the Mormon Church that I blindly believed in – making life decisions based on dogma and tradition that someone years ago had written. I had served the Mormon Church a hundredfold while selling individual creativity down the religious river. Those who feel that quiet inner voice to follow a personal destiny, bravely stand alone in front of an army that wields its swords of judgment. Soaring freedom threatens society's safety of structure and form. Living an individual dream, flying solo, sets off alarms within a closed tribal community, agitating their beauty and oneness that have been crowded out by fear.

A call to conscious action, eyes can now see, ears can hear - shedding the old self, reuniting with the one life that is and always will be, a potential realm of possibility and compassion burning bright as we were destined to. By taking personal responsibility the old patterns of blame no longer have a place. The power of individual choice that awakens our better judgment, manifesting a loving future rather than reliving the past. Forgiveness flows from this perspective allowing empathy to open like a blossoming flower.

I boarded my flight back to my world of isolation. The trip home felt easy and effortless. What was once a driven destination now felt like my home, at least for now. What was once safe was now unsettling; what was once unsettling was now safe. A world of contaminated thought, left behind, leaving me feeling weightless, and open to the world of gifts that came in the form of life. The support I received from strangers flowed into my life like angels that had awaited my arrival. Noticing everyone and everything captured my new childlike rapture of connecting with the right people. People became a gift of beauty and a reflection of my own inner beauty. I saw only beauty in a land that I once viewed as hostile and unsafe.

My story was no longer a story that held me prisoner. It was a path of lessons that were for me and me alone. From my childhood abuse, to the Mormon Church, my resentment and the anger that held me in its grip for so many years, I was finally free to soar in effortless flight with a perspective that blamed no one. Any action that I once perceived to be against me was no longer personal. No one could abuse me but me alone. Laying down my sword of personal abuse and retaliation was effortless. I had discovered that coveting the role of victim served no one; all it led to was a battering of self and a deflection of repeated behavior.

My lessons reflected all that I now viewed as necessary for the evolution of the path that served humanity. What greater purpose could there be for me than helping individuals heal from all the abuse that continues each day, giving them the elevated vision that we can rise above the dysfunction with a new perspective, and teaching a new generation that we believe in love. Masking the pain can only last so long. Waking up the shadows of long-ago pain and facing it head-on allows a space of knowing and accepting. A moment of truth surely outweighs a life of victimhood leading to pain and regret.

Standing up for a cause only serves the cause without serving the whole of humanity. Standing up for yourself can only serve the whole of humanity through your reconnection with it. Showing up for humanity creates a harmonic balance that connects you to the living source that we all come from. When this happens the cause loses its form of self-delusional separation by accepting the truth of who we really are.

My family, who mouthed trust and compassion, were far from taking responsibility – seeking salvation was more important to them than honesty. Finding forgiveness was a path that I alone had to find: I would arrive at its door knocking for an embrace of outstretched arms. My arrival was long-awaited. Holding on to baggage was no longer fit for my journey. I was invited in: the warmth of the fire welcomed me with crackling sounds of freedom. I sat down with belated delight, weary and battered from years of heavy journeying. The divide that had seemed at times far too wide, I had crossed. I curled my body up into my chair. Sitting by the fire melted all the past away; the only moment that mattered was this one. I asked a simple question, whispering it to the flickering flames: Have I let go of my heavy baggage? The flames whispered back, What are you holding on to? I drifted off to sleep with both hands wide open.

Todd Preston is the happy father of five daughters, with another child on the way. He resides in the Bay of Plenty region of New Zealand with his wife Dana and their little girl Raven. After taking three years to write and begin a new life, Todd has returned to his career as a chiropractor. Writing is still a very important aspect of his life; the creative heartbeat and color of words will always stir his soul. In his spare time, sitting close to nature with his sweetheart, a glass of red wine and a good cigar still puts a smile on his face.

www.ingramcontent.com/pod-product-compliance
Lightning Source LLC
Chambersburg PA
CBHW051736040426
42447CB00008B/1159